Changing Lives of
Crime and Drugs

The Wiley Series
in
Offender Rehabilitation

Edited by

Clive R. Hollin
*Rampton Hospital, Nottinghamshire
& University of Leicester, UK*

and

Mary McMurran
*East Midlands Centre for Forensic Mental Health, Leicester,
& University of Leicester, UK*

Changing Lives of Crime and Drugs

Intervening with Substance-Abusing Offenders

Glenn D. Walters

JOHN WILEY & SONS

Chichester · New York · Weinheim · Brisbane · Singapore · Toronto

National   01243 779777
International (+44) 1243 779777
e-mail (for orders and customer service enquiries): cs-book@wiley.co.uk
Visit our Home Page on http://www.wiley.co.uk
or http://www.wiley.com

Other Wiley Editorial Offices

John Wiley & Sons, Inc., 605 Third Avenue,
New York, NY 10158-0012, USA

WILEY-VCH Verlag GmbH, Pappelallee 3, D-69469
Weinheim, Germany

Jacaranda Wiley Ltd, 33 Park Road, Milton,
Queensland 4064, Australia

John Wiley & Sons (Asia) Pte Ltd, 2 Clementi Loop #02-01,
Jin Xing Distripark, Singapore 129809

John Wiley & Sons (Canada) Ltd, 22 Worcester Road,
Rexdale, Ontario M9W IL1, Canada

Library of Congress Cataloging-in-Publication Data

Walters, Glenn D.
  Changing lives of crime and drugs : intervening with substance
  -abusing offenders / Glenn D. Walters.
      p.   cm. — (The Wiley series in offender rehabilitation)
  Includes bibliographical references and index.
  ISBN 0-471-97658-X (cloth). — ISBN 0-471-97841-8 (pbk.)
    1. Narcotic addicts—Rehabilitation.   2. Criminals—
Rehabilitation.   3. Drug abuse—Treatment.   I. Title.   II. Series.
HV5801.W344   1988   97-33964
362.29'186'086927—DC21   CIP

British Library Cataloguing in Publication Data

A catalogue record for this book is available from the British Library

ISBN 0-471-97658-X (cased)
ISBN 0-471-97841-8 (paper)

Typeset in 10/12 Century Schoolbook from the author's disks
by Mathematical Composition Setters Ltd, Salisbury
Printed and bound in Great Britain by Biddles Ltd, Guildford and Kings Lynn
This book is printed on acid-free paper responsibly manufactured from sustainable forestry,
in which at least two trees are planted for each one used for paper production.

Dedication

This book is dedicated to the three people who continue to have the greatest impact on my life—my wife, Patti, and my two children, Christopher and Tara.

Contents

About the Author

Glenn D. Walters received his Ph.D. in Counseling Psychology from Texas Tech University in 1982 and took his predoctoral internship in Clinical Psychology at Dwight David Eisenhower Army Medical Center, Fort Gordon, Georgia. After serving as Chief Psychologist at the United States Disciplinary Barracks, Fort Leavenworth, Kansas, from 1983 to 1984, Dr Walters went to the Federal Bureau of Prisons as a staff psychologist at the United States Penitentiary, Leavenworth, Kansas. It was here that he first developed a substance abuse program for criminal offenders. Since January 1992 Dr Walters has been at the Federal Correctional Institution, Schuylkill, Pennsylvania, where he serves as staff psychologist and co-ordinator of drug abuse programming. The author's research interests center around the study of drugs and crime, and how these two behaviors often form overlapping lifestyles. In working with clients Dr Walters' approach is to encourage client self-confidence through the development of life, thinking, coping, and social skills. Accordingly self-efficacy, skills training, and the client–therapist relationship are of primary concern in his interactions with clients. Dr Walters has previously written books on crime (*The Criminal Lifestyle*, 1990; *Criminal Science* (Vols I & II), 1992), drugs (*Escaping the Journey to Nowhere*, 1994; *Substance Abuse and the New Road to Recovery*, 1996), and the drug–crime connection (*Drugs and Crime in Lifestyle Perspective*, 1994), and regularly conducts workshops on the lifestyle model.

Series Preface

Twenty years ago it is doubtful that any serious consideration would have been given to publishing a series of books on the topic of offender rehabilitation. While the notion of rehabilitation for offenders was widely accepted 30 years ago, the 1970s saw the collapse of what we might call the treatment ideal. As many other commentators have noted, the turning point can be pinpointed to the publication of an article titled "What Works—Questions and Answers about Prison Reform", written by Robert Martinson and published in 1974. The essential message taken from this article was that, when it comes to the rehabilitation of offenders, what works is "nothing works". It would be stretching the case to say that Martinson single-handedly overturned the rehabilitative philosophy, but his message was obviously welcomed by a receptive audience. As writers such as Don Andrews have suggested there are many reasons why both the academic community and politicians and policy-makers were more than willing to subscribe to the "nothing works" philosophy. (Although the evidence suggests that the public at large did not buy completely the need to abandon rehabilitation.) Thus the 1970s and 1980s saw a return to hard sentencing, the predominance of punishment, and the handing out of just deserts to those who transgressed the law of the land. Throughout this period of rehabilitative nihilism a small group of academics and practitioners kept faith with the rehabilitative ideal, led perhaps by Paul Gendreau and Robert Ross, and slowly began to look for new ways to argue the case for rehabilitation. The turnabout, when it came, was dramatic. Through the development of a methodology for statistically reviewing large bodies of research, called "meta-analysis", unequivocal evidence was produced that rehabilitative programmes did work. The view that "nothing works" is simply wrong: rehabilitation programmes do have a positive effect in reducing recidivism. The effect is not always large, although sometimes it is; nor is it always present, although on average it is. However, it is there and that cannot be ignored. Since 1990, armed with these findings, there has been a remarkable resurgence of the rehabilitative ideal: practitioners have eagerly attended conferences, seminars, and training courses; researchers are working not to make the case for rehabilitation, but to improve and refine techniques for working with offenders.

This series aims to provide a reading source of information, for both practitioners and researchers, on the developments as the renewed emphasis on rehabilitative work with offenders gathers pace. We are keenly looking forward to its unfolding, and we hope that in time practitioners and researchers will also eagerly await each new volume.

Mary McMurran
Clive R. Hollin

Preface

Numerous attempts have been made to explain the drug–crime connection. The position argued here is that the drug–crime connection derives from an overlapping relationship that forms between the drug and criminal lifestyles. It is therefore imperative that clinicians address both lifestyles in their interventions with clients. This book begins by challenging four words (unconscious, addiction, treatment, rehabilitation) that have helped shape the views of many professionals working in the mental health, substance-abuse, and criminal justice fields. Chapter 2 provides an overview of traditional and non-traditional explanations of the drug–crime connection, while Chapter 3 scrutinizes major models of intervention. This is followed by a chapter that describes how the drug and criminal lifestyles are properly defined. Tracing the intervention sequence from beginning to end, Chapters 5 through 7 examine the assisted change process partitioned into three phases: foundation, vehicles, and development of a reinforcing non-drug/non-criminal lifestyle. The final chapter of this book explores the issue of application. In this chapter two case studies are used to illustrate the effective utilization of material presented in the previous seven chapters. The goal of this book is to provide a comprehensive interpretation of the relationship that exists between drugs and crime and a practical guide for professionals wishing to intervene with clients who find themselves in the eye of this relationship.

The assertions and opinions contained herein are the private views of the author and should not be construed as official or as reflecting the views of the Federal Bureau of Prisons or United States Department of Justice.

Glenn D. Walters

CHAPTER 1

Drugs and Lifestyle

Having been trained as a cognitive-behavioral psychologist I am intrigued by the words that mark people's descriptions of themselves and others. Words may, in fact, hold the key to understanding such complex issues as drug abuse, crime, and lifestyles because words reflect how a person construes reality, a reality that is invented rather than discovered (Hare-Mustin & Marecek, 1988). Since no two versions of reality are exactly alike, the best we can hope for in communicating among ourselves is a reasonable degree of consensus in our views of people, places, and events. Individuality comes into play in the form of a person's lifestyle or style of life (not to be confused with a drug or criminal lifestyle). The position argued here is that each lifestyle comprises an inner or self-view and an outer or world-view, both of which are shaped by the words people use. Instead of aspiring to identify the "right" way to construe reality, it may be more productive to identify ways of construing reality that are maximally beneficial to ourselves and others. To this end I would like to discuss briefly four words that frequently stand in the way of constructing a reality that optimizes the human organism's adaptive capabilities.

THE UNCONSCIOUS

Sigmund Freud (1961) is generally credited with having directed our attention to the unconscious mind as the primary motivator and organizer of behavior. He believed that the unconscious comprised thoughts, feelings, memories, and impulses that were so threatening to a person's psychological stability and self-concept that they were repressed. Freud asserted that this material was barred from everyday awareness, but found its expression in dreams, slips of the tongue, and signs of psychopathology. Psychoanalysis and the formation of a transference relationship were additional ways Freud believed a therapist might access the unconscious. The topographical model proposed by Freud has unfortunately contributed to a fragmentation of human consciousness in which some regions of the mind are believed to be accessible to conscious awareness but many other areas are seen as closed off. In holding to the primacy of unconscious determinants of behavior, Freud argued that repressed memories played a leading role in our everyday lives. Consciousness and decision-making were all but forgotten in Freud's attempts to map the unconscious mind. Fortunately, this trend has shown signs of reversing itself as dissatisfaction with the psychoanalytic model has mounted. Nevertheless, belief in the unconscious continues to influence people's perceptions on human deportment despite the fact neuropsychological and cognitive studies show that many implicit and "unconscious" expressions are more a function of the ordinary computations and limitations of the human brain than a consequence of affectively charged psychodynamic processes (Schacter, 1994).

It would be untenable to argue that people are aware of all things at all times. Experience has taught us that conscious awareness varies across time and situation. This does not mean, however, that Freud's views on the unconscious are correct or that repression is the primary vehicle by which people forget. In contrast to the psychoanalytic belief in the unconscious, the view espoused in this book is that much of what has been attributed to the unconscious mind actually reflects the information-processing capacities and limitations of the human brain. Memory storage, selective attention, and automatic processing (Cowan, 1988) are just a few of the factors that may account for the differing levels of awareness observed in the human organism. Emotional turmoil can also interfere with one's perception of an event just as proactive and retroactive inhibition limit the richness with which a particular thought is coded, symbolized, and processed. These are not acts of an unconscious mind but the processing limitations of a brain inundated with more information than it can effectively handle. The partial processing of information may be adaptive in the sense that it prevents the individual from becoming overwhelmed by superfluous information. It is only when these limitations and styles obstruct information necessary for effective decision making that they become problematic.

ADDICTION

Originally invented to symbolize the habitual use of mind-altering substances, the term addiction has been applied to an ever-increasing array of behaviors and activities. Problems ranging from marital instability to murder have been blamed on addictions to drugs, gambling, sex, and television. It seems that people are less likely to be held accountable for their actions than they were in the past, a trend that can perhaps be attributed, in part, to the proliferation of interest that has grown up around the addiction concept. In some instances the person is said to have been born with a genetic defect and in other instances an environmental stimulus or event is held to be so powerful that it overrides one's ability to resist the temptation to engage in a negative behavior. Many supporters of the addiction concept believe that people are forced to engage in drug use or gambling because they are caught in a web of addictive influence. Rather than being in control of their actions, people so classified are seen as victims of a process that saps their adaptive energies. Addiction has become a metaphor for the trials and tribulations of modern life and people's alienation from one another. Many have found it easier to surrender to this trend than to search for an alternative. However, by shifting responsibility for their problem behavior onto a putative dependence on alcohol, gambling, or exercise individuals may be relinquishing their personal powers to change. It is no coincidence that the ranks of lawyers and politicians—two groups that may benefit from people's unwillingness to assume responsibility for their actions—have swelled in recent years. Addiction may be a boon for lawyers and politicians, but sets up a self-fulfilling prophesy of depowerment for the rest of us. Walters (1998) makes the additional point that the concept of addiction is beset with a plethora of logical, empirical, and practical problems.

Lifestyles provide one alternative to the concept of addiction. Hence, it may be useful to translate what has traditionally been conceptualized as addiction into lifestyle terms. A lifestyle is defined as a routinized pattern of behavior, similar, at least superficially, to the concept of addiction. There is, however, a fundamental difference between the two concepts. Whereas addiction leaves little room for personal choice, the lifestyle concept is rooted in choice and decision-making. Within the lifestyle model the person is viewed as an active decision-maker who establishes goals and priorities, generates and evaluates life options, and possesses the ability to choose from a range of alternatives. Lifestyles are theoretically defined by the three C's of lifestyle theory: conditions, choice, and cognition. Conditions are those internal and external factors that frequently work their way into theories of addiction. Lifestyle theory treats these conditions, not as major determinants of behavior, but as influences that either enhance or limit a person's life options. As the theory goes, the person selects one or more currently available options and then goes about modifying his or her thinking in an effort to justify or rationalize his or her decisions in life. While addiction theories frequently minimize choice and personal responsibility, the lifestyle model is grounded in human causativity (Bakan, 1996) and the capacity for self-determination.

TREATMENT

Mental health professionals frequently make reference to treating substance abuse as if they were about to apply a medical procedure to a physically ill patient. Psychotherapy, however, is a complicated process; certainly more complicated than removing a cancerous tumor or dispensing a vial of medication. In truth, the power, scope, and efficacy of psychological forms of intervention have been shown to vary as a function of the strength of the client–therapist relationship (Najavits & Strupp, 1994). Some theorists have even argued that the psychotherapist's primary function is to empower clients by buttressing a client's belief in his or her ability to effect change in his or her own life (Walters, 1997b). Equating psychotherapy and medical practice would therefore seem ill-advised. The position adopted in the present book is that substance-abusing offenders are neither sick nor in need of medical attention for their drug-abusing or criminal behavior. In point of fact, the nature and purpose of medical treatment and psychological intervention are in many ways antithetical. Whereas medical procedures tend to be performed on a passive patient, the success of psychotherapeutic intervention rests with the formation of an active collaborative relationship between the therapist and client. Since these two terms describe widely disparate processes, it would seem important that they be kept separate.

As an alternative to treatment, the lifestyle model recommends a focus on change. It is proposed that people change in response to the reality of a constantly changing environment. Since survival is viewed as the ultimate goal of all living organisms, lifestyle theorists conceive of change as the way in which an organism improves its fitness. Adaptive change is believed to be mediated by the respect that people have for themselves, others, and the surrounding environment. Research indicates that most people escape from a drug or criminal lifestyle without benefit of formal intervention (Walters, 1998). These changes, which appear to be largely self-initiated and self-maintained, reflect processes that have been integrated into a program of assisted change known as the lifestyle change model. Given the fact that formal intervention rarely attains the potency of self-change, the lifestyle therapist attempts to tap into the client's own natural reservoir of change vehicles in formulating strategies for intervention. The astute therapist assists and encourages the natural change process rather than forcing a preconceived, and perhaps inappropriate, blueprint onto the client (McMurran, 1994). There is no place in a lifestyle therapist's armamentarium for a cookie-cutter philosophy of intervention. It is for this reason that intervention is individualized and tailored to the client's personal fund of adaptive resources.

REHABILITATION

Rehabilitation, as applied to psychological issues, can be defined as an effort to restore a client to a normal or optimal state of mental health or behavioral adjustment. How, one might ask, can a person who has never been habilitated be rehabilitated? This question may be particularly relevant to clients in the criminal justice system. Instead of demanding that these individuals be rehabilitated, we need to create programs geared toward skill development. Successes have been recorded in programs that instruct criminal offenders (Palmer, 1991) and substance abusers (Platt & Hermalin, 1989) in social, coping, and educational/vocational skills. Cognitive-behavioral problem-solving training, in which the generation and evaluation of alternatives, means–end thinking, and perspective taking are emphasized, lays the foundation for improved generic problem-solving skills, while social skills training addresses more specific behavioral skill deficits (Platt & Hermalin, 1989). Rehabilitation is probably not the proper term to be used in describing change programs for substance-abusing criminal offenders since many such individuals never possessed the requisite social, coping, and work skills in the first place. Unlike the track star who breaks her leg and eventually returns to competitive form after reconstructive surgery and a period of physical rehabilitation, the drug-abusing offender may have no place from whence to return. For this reason skill development is emphasized by proponents of the lifestyle model.

Instead of rehabilitation, lifestyle theorists speak of habilitation and resocialization. Habilitation entails basic skill development of both a general (problem-solving) and specific (assertion with spouse) nature. Resocialization is a term that incorporates skill development but then expands on the habilitation concept. In so doing, resocialization considers the client's wider self- and world-views as well as basic skill development. Resocialization can perhaps best be understood by examining its position relative to socialization. Socialization is the internalization of values, motives, and beliefs derived from a particular culture, subculture, or group—especially as this relates to the assumption of certain social roles. Resocialization, on the other hand, necessitates adoption of new values, motives, and behaviors as a condition of accepting the norms of a new reference group and assuming social roles congruent with these norms. Like socialization, resocialization encompasses skill development and the modification of a person's self- and world-views, the end goal being to solidify one's adaptive position relative to a constantly changing environment. Whereas rehabilitation is focused on returning the client to a mythical prior state of optimal functioning, habilitation is concerned with teaching the client basic skills, and resocialization is primarily interested in reinforcing the client's adaptive resources.

A WORD ABOUT LABELING

People who enter fully into a lifestyle are no different from those who refrain from such activity, at least in terms of their efforts to achieve a sense of belonging, predictability, and purpose in life. The difference between those who do and those who do not embrace a lifestyle is often that the former get lost in the process of achieving these three life tasks so that their goals and values become distorted and unbalanced. A sense of identity, for instance, is a cardinal motivating feature of human behavior. Identity affords a person both purpose and meaning in life. Conversely, a life without meaning has little direction other than that supplied by the blueprint of a lifestyle. Research indicates that the search for identity can both initiate (Zimmer-Hofler & Dobler-Mikola, 1992) and maintain (Stephens & McBride, 1972) drug-use behavior and that relapse is often traceable to a person's unwillingness to let go of an addict or criminal identity (Stephens, 1971). Rather than being a simple matter of semantics, the words and terms we use to describe ourselves and our experiences can have a monumental impact on our identities and behavior. For a change in lifestyle to occur, these identities must be altered and the self-labeling process terminated. Moving from words to action the remaining chapters of this book illustrate how reconceptualizing drug abuse in criminal offenders, as an outgrowth of the overlapping relationship that forms between two related lifestyles, holds greater potential for change than viewing these individuals as driven by unconscious forces, addicted to drugs or crime, amenable to treatment, or in need of rehabilitation.

CHAPTER 2

The Drug–Crime Connection

Several interpretations of the drug–crime connection have been offered in an effort to explain the apparent overlap between substance abuse and crime. Three such interpretations will be entertained in this chapter: epiphenomenal explanations, unidirectional explanations, and bidirectional explanations. The purpose of this chapter is to provide the reader with an overview of these three interpretations and demonstrate how these divergent views can be integrated into a lifestyle theory of drug–crime interactions. First, however, it will be necessary to provide documentation of a relationship between substance abuse and crime.

DOCUMENTING THE PRESENCE OF A DRUG–CRIME RELATIONSHIP

Evidence of a robust drug–crime connection can be found in studies on drug use in criminal populations, crime in substance-abusing populations, and drug use and crime in the general population. Fifty percent of the inmates confined in US prisons in 1991 acknowledged having used illicit substances in the month prior to their arrest and 30% reported that they were under the influence of an illicit drug when they committed the instant offense (Bureau of Justice Statistics, 1992). Likewise, between 51 and 83% of the arrestees in 23 US cities tested positive for an illegal substance (National Institute of Justice, 1996) and 30% of a group of 268 homicide offenders incarcerated in New York state correctional facilities attributed their involvement in the homicide to their use of substances (Spunt, Brownstein, Goldstein, Fendrich, & Liberty, 1995). Females incarcerated in Canada (Biron, Brochu, & Desjardins, 1995) and the USA (Sanchez & Johnson, 1987) report rates of regular marijuana (34–42%), cocaine (37–51%), and heroin (15–29%) usage that are several times higher than that observed in general population females in these two countries. Substance misuse is also a common event in juvenile

offenders, as revealed in a study by Watts and Wright (1990) in which
40–47% of the variance in minor delinquency and 34–59% of the variance
in violent delinquency could be attributed to substance misuse on the part
of Afro-American, Mexican-American, and white youth detention facility residents. Alcohol and illicit drugs may be used separately or in combination, and research indicates that the interaction may be particularly
criminogenic. Hodgins and Lightfoot (1988), for instance, determined that
offenders who abuse illegal substances are the least criminal and offenders
who abuse both alcohol and illegal drugs the most criminal.

Greater-than-average levels of criminality have also been reported in
substance-abusing populations, thereby furnishing additional support for
the existence of a drug–crime connection. In an early study on this issue,
Tuchfeld, Clayton, and Logan (1982) contrasted heavy-drinking junior
and senior high school students with abstinent or moderate-drinking
students and determined that 40% of the heavy drinkers and 15% of the
moderate-drinking/abstinent students reported breaking into a locked
place within the past year, while 63% of the heavy-drinking students and
32% of their moderate-drinking or abstinent peers acknowledged committing a theft within this same time frame. Tuchfeld and coworkers also
compared heavy-drinking adults and abstinent or moderate-drinking
adults on these same two measures (considered over a subject's lifetime)
and found higher levels of self-reported breaking and entering (18% vs.
9%) and theft (56% vs. 37%) in the heavy-drinking group. Increased levels
of criminality have also been observed in substance misusers from Greece
(Kokkevi, Liappas, Boukouvala, Alevizou, Anastassopoulou, & Stefanis,
1993), Australia (Balnfield, 1991), and Switzerland (Modestin & Ammann,
1995). In the Swiss study male inpatients diagnosed with an alcohol or
drug problem were two times more likely to possess a criminal record than
non-drug- and alcohol-abusing inpatients or a group of matched controls.
Female Swiss inpatients diagnosed with an alcohol or drug-abuse problem
were five to nine times more likely to own a criminal record compared to
non-drug- and alcohol-abusing inpatients and matched controls.

Large-scale general population surveys in which questions concerning
the use of substances and criminal activity are presented to subjects are
a third way investigators have probed the putative drug–crime connection. Akers (1984) conducted such a survey in a large group of junior and
senior high school students and uncovered evidence of a significant correlation between substance abuse and non-substance-related delinquent
behavior. After controlling for age, gender, race, marital status, employment, education, and income, Greenfield and Weisner (1995) determined
that lifetime drinking problems predicted self-reported criminal behavior in two general population surveys. Harrison and Gfroerer (1992)
employed the National Household Survey on Drug Abuse to document a

robust relationship between regular drug use and the probability of being booked for a criminal offense. The results reviewed in this section indicate that, regardless of whether the focus is on substance abuse in criminal offenders, crime in substance abusers, or drug use and criminality in general population respondents, a relationship between substance abuse and crime is undeniable. Demonstrating a relationship between drugs and crime is one thing; explaining this relationship is quite another.

EXPLAINING THE DRUG–CRIME RELATIONSHIP

In this section we will consider three general interpretations of the drug–crime connection. The first set of explanations hold that the observed relationship between substance abuse and crime is a consequence of these two variables' common association with one, or more, "third" variables. Because these explanations presume the presence of a non-causal relationship between substance abuse and crime they will be referred to as epiphenomenal. Unidirectional models, on the other hand, establish a causal connection between substance abuse and crime in which substance abuse is viewed as a cause of crime or crime is viewed as a cause of substance abuse. Bidirectional explanations also postulate the existence of a causal relationship between substance abuse and crime but conceive of this bond as reciprocal in nature. Proponents of this view believe that the causal influence of the drug–crime nexus flows in both directions (i.e., from substance abuse to crime and from crime to substance abuse).

Epiphenomenal Explanations

Epiphenomenal explanations of the drug–crime connection hold that the relationship between drugs and crime is spurious, illusory, and non-causal. One possibility is that offenders use intoxication as an excuse for illegal behavior. Another is that the overlap between drugs and crime is a consequence of each variable's common association with one, or more, "third" variables. Fagan, Weis, and Cheng (1990) collected survey data on 665 inner-city youth and ascertained that serious substance abuse was more prevalent and frequent in persons who engaged in serious acts of delinquency. However, the type of drug used (marijuana) was a more powerful correlate of delinquency than the frequency of usage. Fagan and coworkers concluded that substance abuse and delinquency, rather than being causally connected were artificially linked by a third variable. The third variable in this case was identified as a developmental sequence in which substance abuse and crime were viewed as embedded in parallel, yet independent, social networks of etiological influence. This is not the only epiphenomenal explanation of the drug–crime connection available to researchers. Additional possibilities are described below.

Whereas there is little consensus among epiphenomenal theorists as to the variable or variables responsible for the drug–crime relationship, several viable candidates nonetheless exist. Since it has been shown that substance abuse and crime are not equally distributed across age groups, one possibility is that drugs and crime follow similar age progressions. Hirschi and Gottfredson (1983) have shown that property crime peaks between the ages of 14 and 16 and then falls off dramatically from here. A similar pattern has been observed with substance use, although usage peaks a few years after property crime (Harrison & Gfroerer, 1992; Menard & Huizinga, 1989). The similarity in age curves for marijuana use and crime is illustrated in Figure 2.1. A second possibility is that drug abuse and crime/delinquency spring from an underlying pattern of general deviancy (Jessor & Jessor, 1977), a possibility that has received some empirical support (Clapper, Buka, Goldfield, Lipsitt, & Tsuang, 1995; Farrell, Danish, & Howard, 1992). A third possibility, as suggested by Gottfredson and Hirschi (1990), is that drug use and crime are manifestations of low self-control. However, a recent test of Gottfredson and

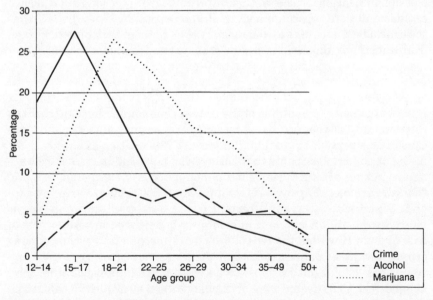

Figure 2.1. Percentage of individuals reporting property crime, marijuana use, and monthly alcohol intoxication within the past year by age. (Source: Harrison, L., & Gfroerer, J., 1992.)

Hirschi's theory found it to be no more useful than traditional models in explaining adolescent drug use (Sorenson & Brownfield, 1995).

Unidirectional Explanations

There are two unidirectional explanations for the drug-crime connection: substance abuse causes crime and crime causes substance abuse. In support of the drugs → crime view, Newcomb and McGee (1989) determined that early alcohol use predicted later delinquency and criminal behavior in both male and female high school students, but that early delinquency had no bearing on later alcohol usage. One way substance abuse may augment the propensity for violent criminality is by adversely effecting a person's mood, judgement, and capacity for self-control. Although alcohol intoxication has been known to promote violence (Green, 1981), the results of at least one study insinuate that violent criminality may be more, rather than less, prominent in offenders testing negative for illegal drugs (Valdez, Kaplan, Curtis, & Yin, 1995). A second possibility is that the high cost of illegal drugs may encourage some people to engage in economically oriented crime as a means of financing their growing drug habit. Harlow (1991), in fact, reports that 13% of the jail inmates he interviewed acknowledged that they had committed their current offense in an effort to secure money to pay for illegal drugs. Longitudinal studies conducted in Baltimore (Ball, Shaffer, & Nurco, 1983), Harlem (Johnson, Goldstein, Preble, Schmeidler, Lipton, Spunt, & Miller, 1985), California (Anglin & Speckart, 1988), and Great Britain (Jarvis & Parker, 1989) tend to confirm this view in demonstrating that heroin usage corresponded with periods of increased economically oriented crime. A third way drugs cause crime is by bringing the drug user into contact with the illicit supply system (Bean & Wilkinson, 1988) or fostering a gradual decline in a person's respect for societal rules (McBride, Burgman-Habermehl, Alpert, & Chitwood, 1986).

The second major unidirectional model holds that crime causes substance abuse (crime → drugs) and is corroborated by research denoting that early antisocial behavior often precedes the use and misuse of alcohol and other substances (Nathan, 1988; Ohannessian, Stabenau, & Hesselbrock, 1995). In fact, a Markov chain analysis of data generated by 431 high rate offenders in Philadelphia revealed that crime-related activities were substantially more likely to culminate in drug-related activities than drug-related behaviors were to culminate in crime (Pettiway, Dolinsky, & Grigoryan, 1994). Drugs, as a case in point, can be used to eliminate internal prohibitions to criminal behavior. In this regard, studies show that burglars frequently consume large amounts of alcohol and other substances prior to committing an offense. This is done in order to ward off and reduce fear, anxiety, and other deterrents to crime (Cromwell, Olson, Avary, & Marks, 1991). Offenders will sometimes also use drugs to celebrate the successful execution of a criminal act. Gibbs and Shelly (1982) observed this in a group of commercial thieves. A third way crime can impact on substance abuse is by increasing the availability of drugs. Faupel (1987) determined that heroin-dependent individuals who had maintained themselves on low–moderate doses of heroin for months increased their intake of opiates following their participation in a lucrative criminal event. The rapid influx of money generated by such crimes made heroin more available to Faupel's subjects, which they then capitalized on by increasing their consumption of heroin. Finally, there is evidence that continued involvement in crime may retard the natural "maturing out" process that often leads to the cessation of drug use in heroin-dependent individuals over time (Anglin, Brecht, Woodward, & Bonett, 1986). The converse can also occur, however, since some studies show that substance abuse is a leading predictor of recidivism in criminal populations (Beck & Shipley, 1989).

Bidirectional Explanations

Bidirectional explanations of the drug–crime relationship reject the simplistic notion that drugs cause crime or that crime causes drugs in favor of the view that drugs and crime are reciprocally related. In other words, drugs and crime are both a cause and effect of one another (drugs ↔ crime). This position has been advanced in Thornberry's (1987) work on reciprocity in delinquency development and in recent studies confirming the presence of a reciprocal relationship between adolescent drug use and such traditional situational indices as parental control (Stice & Barrera, 1995) and peer acceptance (Farrell & Danish, 1993). These findings suggest that substance abuse and crime might also be reciprocally related. Hammersley and Morrison (1987) examined this hypothesis in a series of structured interviews held with 28 active heroin users. The results of this study clearly demonstrate the complexity of the heroin–crime relationship. Heroin use and crime not only interacted with and affected one another, but also appeared to form a relationship that varied in direction and intensity with the introduction of other drugs of abuse like alcohol and tranquilizers. Further confirmation of a bidirectional interpretation of the drug–crime relationship can be found in a three-wave longitudinal panel study by Brook, Whiteman, and Finch (1992). Intercorrelations between early childhood aggression, early and later adolescent delinquency, and drug use showed that early childhood aggression predicted adolescent drug use and that early adolescent drug use predicted later adolescent drug use and delinquency.

AN INTEGRATED MODEL OF DRUG–CRIME INTERACTIONS

Each of the three primary interpretations of the drug–crime connection may explain a portion of the variance shared by substance abuse and crime, but none of these interpretations is capable of accounting completely for the drug–crime nexus. Sometimes the drug–crime relationship can be traced to a third variable, whether a common set of skill deficits, behaviors, or thinking patterns. However, epiphenomenal explanations do not cover all facets of the drug–crime relationship. To the extent that substance abuse is a major cause of isolated criminal events and that crime can sometimes encourage, precipitate, or escalate one's use of substances, unidirectional models also shed light on the drug–crime connection. However, even with epiphenomenal and unidirectional explanations in place, a major portion of the variance in the drug–crime overlap remains unexplained because the relationship is also bidirectional. A longitudinal study conducted on a group of adolescents living in Ontario between 1983 and 1991 not only identified falling levels of drug use and delinquent behavior, but also uncovered a steady decline in the correlation between drug use and delinquency over time (Adlaf, Smart, Walsh, & Ivis, 1994). The reciprocal nature of drug–crime interactions must consequently be included in any serious attempt to explain the drug–crime connection. In an effort to capitalize on the individual strengths of the three major interpretations of drug-crime association, I will attempt to show how these three views can be integrated into a single model using lifestyle theory as a general framework. Because a complete accounting of lifestyle theory is outside the scope of this book, the present discussion restricts itself to three general topics with relevance to the drug–crime connection.

Incentive and Opportunity in Lifestyle Development

Lifestyles are grounded in the incentive (motivation) and opportunity (learning) to engage in patterned behavior. The incentive for lifestyle development is grounded in fear. This fear is believed to be a natural consequence of the conflict that develops between a living organism, equipped with an instinct to survive, and a constantly changing environment that challenges the organism's survival. The ensuing response registers as cellular imbalance in organisms lacking a central nervous system, primal fear in organisms with a central nervous system, and existential fear in organisms that possess both a central nervous system and the capacity for self-awareness. A review of fear and phobia development supplies greater support for a Darwinian (survival/fitness) model of fear acquisition than an associational (learning/conditioning) one (Menzies &

Clarke, 1995). Primal and existential fear, it is argued, can be managed in one of three principal ways. The organism can either make internal changes designed to better meet the demands of a constantly changing environment (adaptation), become overwhelmed by the change (despair), or organize its behavior into routinized patterns (lifestyle). These management styles are not mutually exclusive and most people employ some combination of styles in coping with existential fear. The goal of lifestyle intervention is to increase the amount of time people spend engaged in adaptive pursuits and reduce the amount of time they spend reciting and enacting lifestyle patterns of behavior.

Over time, existential fear becomes an individualized expression of a person's current life situation. Thus, while fear has its origins in the conflict that takes place between the life instinct and a constantly changing environment, it responds to various transforming life experiences. Three categories of experience are particularly important in molding the fear into an individualized expression of a person's current existential condition. Each category of experience relates directly to the issue of survival. The early homo sapiens learned that survival depended largely on the ability to band together into groups. As such, early attachment and social relationships were vital to human survival. Attachment and such social issues as intimacy, commitment, and rejection, in turn, help shape people's self- and world-views. Predicting and controlling the environment is a second way the human organism protects its survival. Consequently, the human species has set out to understand, tackle, and manage the mysteries of the cosmos. Unfortunately, some of these efforts have resulted in outcomes that have been destructive to the individual as well as to the environment. Personal issues emanating out of these experiences configure existential fear around power and control themes. A third experience that helps transform existential fear is that of identity or self-image. Psychologically, the human organism must have a sense of its own existence, identity, and place in the wider society to survive and prosper. Hence, concerns about success, failure, or identity that arise from these experiences also contribute to the changing face of existential fear.

People enact lifestyles in an effort to manage fear. Different lifestyles address different versions of this fear. However, the selection of one lifestyle over another is also influenced by opportunity. One cannot develop a drug lifestyle in an environment where drugs are not available, just as one cannot establish a criminal lifestyle in the absence of salient criminal role models. These experiences and models, whether actual or fantasized, must be present if a lifestyle is to take root. As lifestyles are acquired through socialization, lifestyle-promoting conditions, reinforcers, and role models must be available to the individual if he or she is to have the opportunity to learn the attitudes and behaviors associated with that lifestyle. Owing to the fact that the drug and criminal lifestyle share many of the same underlying features (i.e., an emphasis on short-term gratification and a disregard for the negative long-term consequences of one's behavior) it may very well be that exposure to one lifestyle augments opportunities for acquiring the other lifestyle. The incentive and opportunity features of lifestyle development suggest that the drug–crime connection is due, in large part, to the action of third variables (e.g., similar fear-management methods, related self- and world-views), although remnants of a unidirectional philosophy are evident whenever exposure to one lifestyle leads to participation in the other lifestyle.

Attributions, Expectancies, and the Person × Situation Interaction

Attributions are the beliefs people use to make judgements about the perceived causes of their own behavior and that of others. Attributions vary along at least three dimensions: internal–external, global–specific, and stable–unstable (Weiner, 1974). An internal attribution would ascribe causation to oneself (e.g., will, actions, decisions), whereas an external attribution ascribes causation to forces outside oneself (e.g., luck, fate, environmental conditions). Global attributions credit general factors with causing events, while specific attributions focus on the contextual features as causes of events. Finally, stable attributions anticipate minimal change in the perceived causal conditions, while unstable attributions emphasize the changing nature of these conditions. It is generally recognized that negative outcomes attributed to specific and unstable causes are more conducive to change than ones attributed to global and stable causes. Hence, students who attribute a failing test score to the difficulty of that particular test or to being poorly prepared on the day of the test (specific, unstable attributions) are more apt to improve their performance on the next test than students who attribute a failing test score to the difficulty of the overall course or their own stupidity (global, stable attributions). There is less consensus concerning the relative merit of internal and external attributions in promoting change.

Marlatt and Gordon (1985) use the attribution model to explain relapse in substance abusing clients who view abstinence as the sole criterion for success. Clients bearing strict allegiance to the abstinence doctrine are more apt to interpret a slip or lapse (e.g., drinking at their daughter's wedding) as evidence of an internal, global, stable process (i.e., lack of willpower, reactivation of their disease) than are persons adopting more flexible and realistic goals for recovery. The negative self-statements that surface when a person holding to an abstinence standard violates this standard create tension that the individual may then try to ameliorate through increased drug usage (Marlatt & Gordon, 1985). Accordingly, people who make internal, global, and stable attributions for slips and lapses have a greater propensity for relapse than people who attribute slips to external, specific, and unstable causes. The lifestyle model accepts much of what Marlatt has to say about attributions and relapse but questions the wisdom of encouraging external rather than internal attributions in accounting for the negative consequences of one's lifestyle. Internal attributions, it is argued, can be helpful in fostering a sense of personal responsibility in clients. Since attributions are judgements about the perceived causes of one's own or another's behavior they may have something to offer theories designed to explain the drug–crime connection. For the most part, the attributional model takes a unidirectional path in accounting for the drug–crime association to the extent that substance-abuse attributions sometimes cause crime and criminal attributions sometimes cause substance abuse. However, the attributional approach is also open to epiphenomenal explanations of the drug–crime connection.

Expectancies are people's subjective appraisals of what they expect to occur should they engage in a particular behavior. Research indicates that expectancies can be either proximal (immediate) or distal (delayed) and that they impact directly on behavior as well as mediate the effect of other variables on behavior (Greenbaum, Brown, & Friedman, 1995). A drug expectancy might center on the belief that "alcohol will reduce my inhibitions and make me popular," whereas a criminal expectancy anticipates "power, wealth, and respect" through crime. Expectancies generally follow a unidirectional path in accounting for the drug–crime connection but, like attributions, are also subject to epiphenomenal interpretation. Whereas expectancies for drug use may contribute to crime and expectancies for crime may contribute to drug use, these expectancies can also be viewed as epiphenomenally linked by virtue of the fact that they emphasize the short-term positive outcomes of drug use and crime while disregarding the negative long-term consequences. One study in which expectancies for hostility under conditions of alcohol intoxication were found to predict drug dependence serves as a model of how one might adopt a unidirectional view of the drug–crime relationship (Walter, Nagoshi, Muntaner, & Haertzen, 1990). Although expectancies for hostility when intoxicated failed to correlate with measures of antisocial personality, impulsivity, and criminality, they did predict alcohol, marijuana, and opiate abuse. Hence, expectancies for aggressiveness appeared to correlate better with measures of subsequent drug use than with measures of criminality, despite the greater thematic similarity of aggressiveness and crime.

Psychologists and biologists have traditionally focused on the dispositional features of human deportment as manifest in studies on personality and heredity. Sociologists, on the other hand, have traditionally been interested in identifying the environmental or situational parameters of human activity. Lifestyle theory, while not ignoring the role of dispositional and situational factors in explanations of human behavior, is drawn to the interactions that form between dispositional and situational influences. Attributions, expectancies, and even existential fear can be viewed as products of person × situation interaction. Just as dispositional factors interact with sundry environmental conditions to create attributions and expectancies, the innate will to survive (disposition) interacts with a constantly changing environment (situation) to create primal and existential fear. The opportunity (learning) and incentive (existential fear) aspects of lifestyle development are subsequently linked by the integrating action of deep ("drugs will remove all of my insecurities") and surface ("drugs make me popular") expectancies. With respect to the drug–crime connection, dispositional and situational factors lend themselves to a unidirectional interpretation of behavior, whether this involves substance abuse and crime or any other two variables. Interactive variables are more conducive to a bidirectional explanation in that they assume the presence of a reciprocal relationship between variables. This will be elaborated upon further in the next section of this chapter.

The Initiation and Maintenance of Lifestyles

There are three categories of influence important in the evolution of a lifestyle. The first category, vulnerability or predisposing variables, puts the individual at risk for future lifestyle involvement. These variables are typically either dispositional (e.g., genetics, temperament) or situational (e.g., family, poverty) in nature, although person × situation interactions can also place a person at risk for future substance misuse or criminality. A second group of influences viewed to be instrumental in lifestyle development are referred to as initiating or precipitating variables. These are the factors that initiate a person's involvement in drug or criminal activity. Initiating factors are generally either situational or interactive in nature. Maintenance factors are a third set of variables used to explain the evolution of a lifestyle. These factors are typically interactive and encourage a pattern of self-reinforcing behavior that often becomes independent of the predisposing and precipitating factors that originally gave rise to the behavior. Initiating and maintaining factors are not necessarily independent since an initiating factor can sometimes serve a maintaining function. However, it is speculated that, in a majority of cases, initiating and maintaining factors are functionally autonomous. What this means is that even if we can identify and correct the factors that have initiated lifestyle involvement, the behavioral patterns will remain intact until the factors that are maintaining the behavior are also addressed.

Lifestyle theory acknowledges the importance of all three sets of variables in the evolution of a drug or criminal lifestyle, but is chiefly concerned with maintaining factors since these variables presumably give birth to patterned behavior. From the standpoint of lifestyle theory, maintaining factors and their behavioral sequela are the lifestyle. It is speculated that people who enter a lifestyle experience an escalating level of behavioral similarity over time because of the growing influence of maintaining factors and their tendency to enter into reciprocal relationships with one another. Maintaining factors soon become the driving force behind lifestyle involvement, and no matter what people's reasons are for initial involvement in drug use or crime they ultimately engage in these activities because these activities become reinforcing in and of themselves. As such, people coming from very different walks of life who started using drugs or committing crime for widely divergent reasons demonstrate increased behavioral similarity over time due to the growing influence of maintaining factors. A similar progression may mark the relationship that forms between the drug and criminal lifestyles and it is predicted that the overlap that exists between substance abuse and crime should expand as a person's involvement in one of these activities increases. Hence, rising levels of criminality may be met by growing involvement in substance abuse, while decreasing levels of substance abuse may coincide with declining criminal involvement. The growing relationship presumed to exist between the drug and criminal lifestyles is shown in Figure 2.2, which reveals an ever-expanding overlap between substance abuse (left

Top

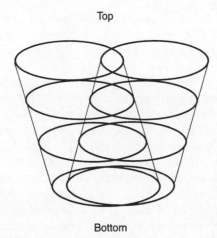

Bottom

Figure 2.2. Three-dimensional representation of the growing overlap that forms between the drug and criminal lifestyles in moving from an early (Top) to a later (Bottom) stage of lifestyle involvement

circle) and crime (right circle) as the person becomes increasingly more involved in one or both lifestyles.

Whereas vulnerability and initiating factors lend themselves to an epiphenomenal or unidirectional interpretation of the drug–crime connection, maintaining factors suggest a reciprocal–interactive perspective in accounting for the relationship that most researchers now agree exists between substance abuse and crime. It has been argued in this chapter that maintaining factors form a dynamic system of interacting variables and conditions. The evolution of this system, as portrayed in Figure 2.2, provides a clear example of how one might conceive of a bidirectional interpretation of the drug–crime relationship. What this diagram and discussion imply is that maintaining factors help establish a reciprocal relationship between drugs and crime that keeps these behaviors locked in a system of self-reinforcing cyclic patterns.

The overriding purpose of this chapter has been to illustrate how the patterned behavior of a lifestyle or the joining of two lifestyles are a consequence of multiple processes (epiphenomenal, unidirectional, and bidirectional) and that while these processes are not reducible to one another they can be organized into a unified and coherent system of theoretical understanding. In an effort to clarify these processes further, Chapter 3 will provide an overview of epiphenomenal, unidirectional, and bidirectional methods of change and offer suggestions as to how these disparate views might be integrated into a workable model of clinical intervention.

CHAPTER 3

Models of Intervention

In the best of all worlds intervention flows from theory. This, unfortunately, does not always occur in our less-than-perfect world, particularly when it comes to substance abuse and crime. It is still possible, nonetheless, to identify intervention strategies that embody the three major theoretical interpretations of drug–crime relationship. Psychoanalysis and behavior therapy, for instance, illustrate how an epiphenomenal approach might be used in one's interventions with substance-abusing offenders. The twelve-step and criminal justice models of intervention, on the other hand, appear to emanate out of a unidirectional interpretation of the drug–crime connection. Finally, the therapeutic community approach to intervention and the matching perspective take a bidirectional view of the drug–crime association. Following a brief review of these six approaches to intervention, an integrated model of therapeutic change will be presented.

THE EPIPHENOMENAL APPROACH TO INTERVENTION

Since epiphenomenal theories assume that the drug–crime connection is traceable to a third variable with which drugs and crime share a common relationship, clinicians operating out of the epiphenomenal perspective seek to identify and confront this third variable. Psychoanalytic theory, for instance, assumes that substance abuse and crime are symptoms of underlying emotional turmoil. Proponents of the psychoanalytic perspective maintain that crime is an unconscious projection of guilt for which the individual seeks atonement by putting himself or herself in a position to be punished (Glover, 1960). Substance abuse is also viewed as having deep-seated emotional origins by theorists and clinicians espousing a psychoanalytic view of human behavior. The self-medication hypothesis is one of the more popular versions of the psychoanalytic approach to substance misuse. This hypothesis holds that the drug-dependent individual consumes chemical substances in an effort to eradicate guilt, depression, and other uncomfortable feelings with origins in major ego deficits (Khantzian, 1985). The psychodynamic therapist attempts to ease the underlying emotional issues that link substance abuse with crime by creating a transference relationship and interpreting the client's behavior in ways that establish a forum wherein clients might learn to work through personal conflicts. There is, however, little empirical support for the theoretical underpinnings or outcome efficacy of psychoanalytic interventions with substance-abusing or non-substance-abusing criminal offenders (Walters, 1992).

The behavioral model also follows an epiphenomenal path in its interpretation of the drug–crime connection. Unlike the psychoanalytic model, which seeks to address deep-seated emotional issues, the behavioral model is nearly exclusively concerned with observable behavior. Assertive (Miller & Eisler, 1977) and social (Monti, Abrams, Binkoff, & Zwick, 1986) skill deficits have been recorded in groups of alcohol-dependent subjects. A variety of social skill liabilities have also been uncovered in delinquent and criminal populations (Ross & Fabiano, 1985). The goal of behavioral intervention, accordingly, is to identify and remedy social-coping skill deficits that link substance abuse to crime or are unique to either behavior. This can be accomplished by implementing a training protocol in which the skill is modeled and discussed, clients are provided an opportunity to practice the skill, feedback is supplied by the therapist and/or other group members, and roadblocks to successful performance of the skill (e.g., anxiety) are removed. Cognitive-behavioral theorists also take an epiphenomenal view of the drug–crime connection but address cognitive skill deficits as well as behavioral skill deficits. Techniques like rational restructuring, self-regulation, and imaginal coping are afforded a prominent position in the cognitive-behavioral therapist's armamentarium of intervention strategies. Unlike the psychoanalytic approach, skills training has been found efficacious with both substance-abusing and non-substance-abusing criminal offenders (Walters, 1992).

THE UNIDIRECTIONAL APPROACH TO INTERVENTION

Unidirectional interpretations of the drug–crime connection maintain that there is a direct causal link between drugs and crime: either drugs cause crime or crime causes drugs. The twelve-step philosophy of Alcoholics Anonymous (AA), which served as the pattern for the twelve steps of Narcotics Anonymous (NA), Cocaine Anonymous (CA), and Marijuana Anonymous (MA), are reproduced in Table 3.1.

Twelve-step programs assume that substance abuse creates negative consequences for the person, one of which is criminal involvement. In

Table 3.1. The twelve steps of Alcoholics Anonymous

1. We admitted we were powerless over alcohol—that our lives had become unmanageable.
2. Came to believe that a Power greater than ourselves could restore us to sanity.
3. Made a decision to turn our will and our lives over to the care of God *as we understood Him*.
4. Made a searching and fearless moral inventory of ourselves.
5. Admitted to God, to ourselves, and to another human being the exact nature of our wrongs.
6. Were entirely ready to have God remove all these defects of character.
7. Humbly asked Him to remove our shortcomings.
8. Made a list of all persons we had harmed, and became willing to make amends to them all.
9. Made direct amends to such people whenever possible, except when to do so would injure them or others.
10. Continued to take personal inventory and when we were wrong promptly admitted it.
11. Sought through prayer and meditation to improve our conscious contact with God, *as we understood Him*, praying only for knowledge of His will for us and the power to carry that out.
12. Having had a spiritual awakening as the result of these steps, we tried to carry this message to alcoholics, and to practice these principles in all our affairs.

The twelve steps are reprinted with permission of Alcoholics Anonymous World Services, Inc. Permission to reprint the twelve steps does not mean that AA has reviewed or approved the contents of this publication, nor that AA agrees with the views expressed herein. AA is a program of recovery from alcoholism *only*— use of the twelve steps in connection with programs and activities which are patterned after AA, but which address other problems, or in any other non-AA context, does not imply otherwise.

taking a unidirectional approach to the drug–crime connection, twelve-step programs base their interventions on the presumption that law-abiding behavior will increase as drug use decreases. The goal of most twelve-step programs is to create an atmosphere of honesty and support in which participants confront the self-defeating nature of their actions, learn to take responsibility for their conduct, and achieve sobriety (Kurtz, 1990). Members are encouraged to select a senior member as a sponsor with whom they might discuss personal feelings, problems, and issues. Even though they run the risk of becoming substitute dependencies, twelve-step programs can be helpful to people committed to change, particularly during the early stages of recovery. Whereas twelve step-programs do not ordinarily lend themselves to empirical evaluation, there is preliminary evidence that in some circumstances they may be more effective than professional treatment (Emrick, Lassen, & Edwards, 1977; Vaillant, 1983).

The criminal justice model asserts that substance abusers, especially those who use illegal substances are, first and foremost, law violators. As such, their rule-breaking behavior must be addressed and, if possible, rectified through forced or mandatory "treatment." Incarceration is viewed by proponents of this model as an intervention unto itself because it removes the individual from the drug-infested environment that has helped maintain his or her drug lifestyle. Anecdotally, at least, some inmates willingly admit that their behavior on the streets was unmanageable and that coming to prison saved their lives. Unfortunately, there are just as many, if not more, prisoners who perpetuate and fine tune their drug lifestyles while in prison. Certain correctional facilities have greater problems with drugs than others, but no prison can lay claim to being entirely drug-free. If drugs are not being smuggled into the institution by visitors or corrupt staff, then they are being manufactured inside the prison walls. It is not uncommon to find inmates brewing their own version of bootleg wine with whatever rotting fruit they can find. Something besides incarceration or separation from a drug-infested environment is therefore required before long-term change can become a reality. The modified criminal justice model seeks to provide psychological services as part of the criminal justice intervention. Such referrals are made routinely as part of a program known as Treatment Alternatives to Street Crime (TASC), the results of which indicate that criminal justice involvement may keep clients in treatment longer than they might otherwise remain, while simultaneously interrupting drug and criminal careers (Hubbard, Collins, Rachal, & Cavanaugh, 1988).

THE BIDIRECTIONAL APPROACH TO INTERVENTION

A bidirectional view of drug–crime intercorrelations, as with the unidirectional perspective, presumes the existence of a causal nexus between these two variables. However, unlike the unidirectional practitioner, the bidirectional theorist maintains that the causal relationship extends in both directions (i.e., from drugs to crime and from crime to drugs). Family systems theory obviously takes a bidirectional view of human behavior, but an even better example of a reciprocal model of drug–crime interrelationships can be found in the therapeutic community approach to intervention. A therapeutic community (TC) is a residential unit in which a variety of interventions are offered and where members take an active role in the daily activities of the unit. TCs can be housed in a correctional center (like the Stay'n Out program in New York) or non-correctional custodial facility (like the Cornerstone Program in Oregon), but are self-contained units isolated from the general inmate population or surrounding correctional/custodial environment. Research has shown modest positive gains in persons completing the Stay'n Out (Wexler, Falkin, Lipton, &

Rosenblum, 1992) and Cornerstone (Field, 1992) programs relative to groups of matched and non-matched controls. Therapeutic communities housed in county jails (where the average length of program involvement is only 54–113 days) have also produced positive results (Tunis, Austin, Morris, Handyman, & Bolyard, 1996). De Leon (1989) notes that approximately 40% of the clients who graduate from TCs exhibit reduced levels of drug use and crime upon release, whereas another 30% display minor improvements. The duration of participation in a TC has been found to predict favorable outcomes (Condelli & Hubbard, 1994), although this may simply reflect the fact that more motivated inmates are less apt to drop out of the program and more apt to remain drug- and crime-free upon release.

A bidirectional perspective is also espoused by clinicians who seek to match clients with interventions. Instead of providing all clients with the same intervention, this approach holds that clients should be paired with interventions that take into account their individual strengths and weaknesses. A review of 21 controlled studies on matching revealed clear evidence in support of the matching hypothesis (Hodgins & Lightfoot, 1988). In the only study of this type to consider substance abuse in criminal offenders, Annis and Chan (1983) determined that high self-esteem alcohol- and drug-abusing offenders enrolled in an 8-week confrontation group therapy program experienced reduced levels of recidivism one year after release relative to a group of inmates who received regular institutional care. Substance-abusing offenders with low self-esteem enrolled in this same group, however, experienced poorer outcomes than the control group of inmates receiving regular institutional care. A prime consideration in conducting matching research is selecting the variable or variables on which clients should be classified and assigned to conditions. Efforts are currently underway to study this issue with respect to clients enrolled in three divergent treatment modalities (Project MATCH Research Group, 1993). The matching hypothesis takes a bidirectional view of the drug–crime relationship in that it is based on the belief that numerous factors, including the interaction that occurs between substance abuse and crime, need to be taken into account when assigning clients to specific interventions. The objective of matching, then, is to identify the intervention that will provide maximum benefit to the client and avoid forcing the client into a monolithic "one size fits all" treatment philosophy.

AN INTEGRATED MODEL OF INTERVENTION

The lifestyle approach to intervention borrows from the six perspectives delineated above in offering an integrated model of intervention.

Psychoanalytic theory's contributions to the lifestyle model include its accent on underlying issues and its emphasis on the client–therapist relationship. Behavioral principles have also contributed to development of a lifestyle model of intervention. Following the lead of behavioral therapists, lifestyle practitioners invest heavily in behavioral and cognitive-behavioral skills training. Congruent with the aims of twelve-step programs, lifestyle therapists stress the necessity of considering substance-abuse issues and providing clients with social support. The criminal justice model reminds therapists to consider the issue of crime in their interventions with clients and the necessity of removing the client from a drug-infested environment as a prelude to change. For optimal results steps should also be taken to limit the client's contact with criminally oriented environments (i.e., general prison population). This, along with efforts to provide clients with increased control over the intervention process, are emphases which the lifestyle model borrows from the therapeutic community approach to intervention. Finally, the lifestyle paradigm insists that intervention be individualized, an affirmation it shares with the matching perspective. What follows is a brief overview of the three primary tenets of the lifestyle approach to intervention.

Laying a Foundation for Change

Change often begins with a crisis, but before a crisis can produce results the person must have confidence in his or her ability to change. Much of the lifestyle therapist's effort, particularly during the early phases of intervention, is spent establishing an alliance with the client designed to bolster the latter's self-confidence. Lifestyle theorists argue that a strong therapeutic alliance has many similarities to the client–shaman relationship found in hunting and gathering societies. As such, mythical constructions may be as vital to the formation of a therapeutic alliance as they are in the construction of a client–shaman bond. Lifestyle theory attributes the non-specific variance normally credited to therapist and relationship factors in outcome research on psychotherapy to a process known as the shaman effect. This is a concept reminiscent of the placebo effect referred to in the psychopharmacological literature. Through interpretation, empathy, and prediction a therapist demonstrates sensitivity to a client's inner world. This, coupled with effective use of positive ritual, metaphor, dialectical methods, and the attribution triad—which consists of a belief in the necessity of change, a belief in the possibility of change, and a belief in one's ability to effect change (Walters, 1996c)—establishes the necessary and sufficient conditions for creation of a shaman effect (Walters, 1997b). Like its psychopharmacological cousin, the shaman effect may be linked to the release of endorphins brought on by the positive outcome expectancies of anticipating help from a knowledgeable and committed shaman or psychotherapist (Shipley, 1988). This effect is designed to empower the client by instilling responsibility, hope, and confidence. The therapist can achieve these goals by emphasizing the aforementioned components of the shaman effect and granting the client increased control over the intervention process.

Lifestyle theory rejects many of the assumptions of psychoanalytic theory but shares the latter's interest in underlying issues. Existential fear, as was mentioned in the previous chapter, has its origins in the conflict that forms when the organism's natural life instinct comes into contact with the uncertainty of a constantly changing environment. The fear can sometimes be managed through institution of a shaman effect and development of basic social, coping, and life skills. When it cannot, the fear must be addressed directly. Unlike the psychoanalytic therapist, the lifestyle practitioner is not principally concerned with deep-seated issues; but unlike the behavioral clinician, the lifestyle practitioner is willing to entertain these issues when it becomes apparent that they play a critical role in the client's current difficulties. Two consequences of existential fear are typically addressed in therapy with clients. The first consequence is escape. People committed to a drug or criminal lifestyle are attempting to escape from fear by constructing a wall of patterned behavior which gives them a false sense of immutability or sameness. The irony is that this illusion of immutability actually sets the stage for the eventual realization of the person's worst fears. As the negative long-term consequences of the person's lifestyle begin to accumulate, the person becomes increasingly more rigid and progressively less adaptable in his or her behavior. In an effort to reduce the mounting tension brought on by a lack of attention to existential fear the individual may seek a palliative, the second consequence or manifestation of existential fear that may surface in therapy sessions with substance-abusing criminal offenders. Since one is no more likely to find a palliative for fear than escape the fear altogether, this too creates substantial problems for the client. These issues are elaborated upon further in Chapter 6 of this text.

Skill Development

Skill development is an essential ingredient of lifestyle intervention. Skills are particularly important in teaching clients how to make better decisions, because the two primary features of decision-making therapy—option expansion and competency enhancement—are skills that can be taught to clients without extensive prior preparation or probing psychodynamic investigation. Clients can also be taught the skills necessary to manage many of the conditions that confront them. Conditions that can be managed with skills training include stress, cues, availability, interpersonal pressure, and existential fear. All but the final condition can be handled through behavioral and cognitive-behavioral skills training. Even existential fear responds to behavioral and cognitive-behavioral programming (through increased self-efficacy) although, as was mentioned previously, it may be necessary to go beyond behavioral and cognitive-behavioral skills training to get at the roots of this particular condition. There is a third area in which skills training can be helpful in confronting the cognitive parameters of lifestyle development, especially the thinking patterns that protect the lifestyle from the reality of a person's current life situation. Cognitive skills for which recognized intervention strategies currently exist include rational restructuring, cognitive relabeling, self-maintenance, and self-regulation. Lifestyle theory, it would seem, owes a debt of gratitude to the behavioral and cognitive-behavioral schools of thought in its use of skill-based methods of intervention. Despite this positive review, skills training is no panacea. As a case in point, Hawkins, Catalano, Gillmore, and Wells (1989) determined that residential drug program participants randomly assigned to a 10-week supplemental behavioral skills training course exhibited superior social-coping skills 12 months after training in comparison to residents receiving no such training, but that there were few training-control differences in subsequent drug use.

The lifestyle therapist eschews the practice of forcing clients into a preconceived program of intervention. Skills are evaluated, after which training is identified for those skills on which the client demonstrates a deficiency. It makes no more sense to train a client in a skill he or she already possesses than base an intervention on a skill the client obviously lacks. Lifestyle intervention is tailored to the individual strengths and weaknesses of the identified client; capitalizing on strengths and alleviating weaknesses. However, with substance-abusing criminal offenders both drug and criminal issues need to be addressed. The specific issues may vary from client to client, but the general categories of drugs and crime should be considered since in many cases both patterns, regardless of which one developed first, are active. Therefore, in situations where the intervention is directed at only one of the two lifestyles, the neglected lifestyle may wind up acting as a trigger for the addressed lifestyle. This is manifest, not only in substance abusers who fail to mature out of their drug lifestyle because of their continued involvement with crime (Anglin, Brecht, Woodward, & Bonett, 1986) but also in criminal offenders who recidivate because of their ongoing misuse of substances (Beck & Shipley, 1989). Lifestyle intervention rejects the "cookie cutter" or "one size fits all" philosophy of many institutionalized programs and allows for the possibility that clients are individuals who may do better with one type of intervention than another. In point of fact, the notion of a blueprint is often what drives a drug or criminal lifestyle. The approach espoused in this book, on the other hand, honors the dignity of the human being and proposes that the paths people follow in exiting a lifestyle are as unique as the paths that led them into the lifestyle in the first place.

Resocialization

Research intimates that a sizeable proportion of people abandon a drug (Biernacki, 1990) or criminal (Hare, McPherson, & Forth, 1988) lifestyle without benefit of formal intervention. This has been variously referred to as burnout, maturity, and natural recovery. Unassisted change will be the term used in this book to describe desistance from a lifestyle without professional intervention (McMurran, 1994). The point made by research on natural recovery is that change is a process rather than an event—a process that may or may not involve a program of formal intervention. One major objective of lifestyle theory is to identify the factors involved in the initiation and maintenance of the unassisted change process. A second major objective is to determine how these factors can be effectively integrated into a program of assisted change. Numerous variables have been identified in the research literature, three of which assume a prominent position in the present model. Initially, clients are encouraged to change their involvements; in other words, they are asked to modify their daily routines, activities, and interpersonal relationships. Then, clients must alter their commitments and priorities by reorganizing goals, values, and priorities. Unless values and associations change the person is likely to revert to patterns with which he or she is familiar. Finally, the client must implement a new identity or risk returning to a former lifestyle in an attempt to recapture the identity once provided by this lifestyle. Lifestyles, as the reader may recall, are learned through a process of socialization. Whatever has been learned can be unlearned, but unlearning often leaves a void. This void must be filled with a reasonable alternative lifestyle or the individual will tend to revert to old patterns.

Creating an alternative lifestyle requires activation of the resocialization process wherein the client finds involvements, commitments, and identities incompatible with the continued misuse of substances and habitual violation of societal rules. The success of the resocialization process often depends on the amount of social support a person receives. Studies indicate that one of the strongest predictors of long-term positive outcome in former substance abusers (Booth, Russell, Soucek, & Laughlin, 1992; Higgins, Budney, Bickel, & Badger, 1994), delinquents (Hammersley, Forsyth, & Lavelle, 1990), and adult offenders (Clark,

1992) is a reliable network of conventional social support. In the absence of familial support, alternative avenues of social support must be identified. A twelve-step fellowship provides each new member with a sponsor to whom he or she can turn as a source of guidance and support. The results of one study, in fact, insinuate that social support from friends and family had little bearing on whether or not a group of female substance abusers completed a halfway-house program for chemically dependent women. On the other hand, the quantity and quality of the social support these women received from their Alcoholics Anonymous (AA) sponsors was a robust predictor of program completion (Huselid, Self, & Gutierres, 1991).

Since resocialization necessitates development of an alternate lifestyle the individual must be motivated to find this new lifestyle. Abandoning old patterns is only the first step in the change process. So that the change might be maintained, initial desistance from a lifestyle must be reinforced with a suitable alternate lifestyle in which goals, values, and relationships incompatible with the old lifestyle are erected. This requires resocialization—a process which rests heavily on a person's natural reservoir of social support.

CHAPTER 4

Defining the Drug and Criminal Lifestyles

In order to avoid the circular reasoning that appears to afflict the behavioral (Gorman, 1989) and twelve-step (Heather & Robertson, 1985) interpretations of the drug–crime connection, the lifestyle perspective has introduced two distinct models: a descriptive or structural model and an explanatory or functional model. The descriptive model considers the structure of lifestyles in an attempt to assemble a working definition of the behavioral patterns found in a lifestyle, whereas the explanatory model outlines the proposed nature and function of lifestyle activity. The two models were designed to be complementary, but it is possible to use one without the other or for one to be valid and the other not. The goal of this chapter is to present a brief description of the drug and criminal lifestyles and other major structural elements of lifestyle theory. While a comprehensive presentation of the functional model is beyond the scope of this book, a brief synopsis is provided in Chapter 2. In order that the reader might appreciate lifestyle structure it is imperative that the three C's and four R's of lifestyle theory be fully understood. Accordingly, these particular structural elements of lifestyle theory will be examined first, followed by a review of the defining characteristics of the drug and criminal lifestyles.

THE THREE C's AND FOUR R's OF LIFESTYLE THEORY

The Three C's

The three C's of lifestyle theory are the framework upon which specific lifestyles are erected. These three factors—conditions, choice, and cognition—are believed to interact in such a way as to produce the behavioral styles that define a drug or criminal lifestyle. The first C, which stands for conditions, covers the internal and external influences that either increase or decrease a person's risk of becoming involved in a particular pattern of behavior. Conditions consequently function along a risk–protection continuum. Some categories of genetic-temperamental disposition elevate a person's chances of becoming involved in criminal behavior or substance abuse, whereas other categories of genetic-temperamental disposition appear to lower a person's propensity for criminal or drug involvement. Likewise, certain familiar-environmental milieus make it more likely that a person will take advantage of future drug or criminal opportunities, while other familiar-environmental milieus reduce drug and criminal opportunities. Internal and external risk and protective factors form an intricate web of cross-socializing influences that exert a profound effect on behavior. In fact, the variance attributable to person × situation interaction may be even greater than that normally attributed to individual person and situation variables, whether the subject is crime (Hanson, Henggeler, Haefele, & Rodick, 1984) or substance abuse (Jessor, Van Den Bos, Vanderryn, Costa, & Turbin, 1995).

Despite the powerful effect conditions wield over behavior, they do not cause behavior directly. Instead, conditions act to increase (protective effect) or decrease (risk effect) a person's options in life, from whence the person makes a decision. This is where the second of the three C's comes into play. From the options available to him or her at any particular point in time, the person makes a choice. It should be noted that these mental operations need not be optimal to qualify as choices. More often than not, people select the options that seem most expedient or were successful the last time they found themselves in a similar predicament. Lifestyle theory asserts that people are active decision makers who generate, evaluate, and select options and alternatives and evidence in support of this supposition is imbedded in research on substance misuse (Bennett, 1986) and crime (Weaver & Carroll, 1985). Choice can also be viewed as a manifestation of non-linear processes through which small fluctuations in behavior eventually become amplified to create new behaviors that are not fully deducible from knowledge of previous conditions (Krippner, 1994). Hence, even if scientists were to have all the relevant conditional data at their fingertips and knew precisely how to use this information, they would still not be in a position to make flawless predictions of behavior. This is because choice and decision making render an unrestricted positivistic view of human deportment obsolete.

Cognition is the third of the three C's. The major difference between the mental operations that constitute the second and third C's is that the thinking referenced in the latter is less circumscribed than that which defines the former. Cognition follows two primary pathways: one of which is constructional, the other defensive. Lifestyle theory concurs with social constructionalist arguments that there is no such thing as objective reality and that each person constructs his or her own reality (Gergen, 1985). According to lifestyle theory, there are four primary avenues of reality construction. The mythical method is based on the strength of conviction and belief, the empirical method on empirical observation, the teleological method on goals, and the epistemological method on sensitivity to the inherent limitations of the other methods. By reason of perception, attention, and limited storage (all second C mental operations) this process is frequently implicit (Stacy, Ames, Sussman, & Dent, 1996), although not necessarily unconscious. This leads to the construction of a belief system which the individual seeks to defend. Defense can be accomplished through denial (incongruous/irrelevant information is either not acknowledged or not symbolized), distortion (incongruous information is modified), diversion (responsibility for an experience is externalized, displaced, or inverted), or justification (incongruous information is reinterpreted or congruous information is applied). Constructional and defensive cognitions often interact. There are many consequences to this interaction, one of the more prominent being lifestyle-supporting thinking styles (see Chapter 6 for a complete description of these thinking styles).

One way to conceptualize the three C's is as a system of interacting influences in which conditions set the parameters of the choices the individual makes and cognitions come into the picture as the person attempts to justify and reinforce his or her choices. However, human behavior is rarely this simple. Choice and cognition may have as much impact on conditions as conditions have on the mental operations of choice and cognition. It might reasonably be anticipated, then, that the correlations between these three factors are more often reciprocal than unidirectional. The interdependency and reciprocity that forms between the three C's is viewed to be the driving force behind the behavioral styles or defining characteristics of a lifestyle. Why a lifestyle unfolds rather than a more adaptive alternative or why one lifestyle surfaces instead of another are questions addressed by the functional model. The descriptive or structural model is more concerned with what the behavioral styles are than with explaining how they might have developed. For this reason, the descriptive model is used to define the drug and criminal lifestyles. A critical assumption made by the descriptive model of lifestyle theory is that behavioral styles assume the form of continua rather than discrete dichotomies. Before describing the behavioral styles that define the drug and criminal lifestyles, mention needs to be made of four additional features of lifestyle structure—namely, the four R's.

The Four R's

Whereas the interactive relationship that forms between the three C's furnishes a framework for lifestyle structure, the four R's supply much of the content of the defining behavioral styles. Each lifestyle has it own rules, roles, rituals, and relationships—the four R's of lifestyle theory. The four R's flesh out the behavioral patterns that define a lifestyle. Rules are the regulations that guide enactment of a behavioral style. Roles are the prescribed parts a person plays in performing a behavioral style. Rituals are the routinized patterns of conduct into which a behavioral style falls. Relationships are the social interactions a person entertains as part of a behavioral style. A representative sampling of rules, roles, rituals, and relationships found in the behavioral styles for the criminal and drug lifestyle are listed in Tables 4.1 and 4.2, respectively. Since multiple rules, roles, rituals, and relationships exist for each behavioral style, the structural elements listed in these two tables are clearly not exhaustive. Nevertheless, they do afford the reader a general overview of the types of rules, roles, rituals, and relationships found in the behavioral styles of a criminal or drug lifestyle.

Table 4.1. Sample rules, roles, rituals, and relationships of a criminal lifestyle

Behavioral characteristic	Rules	Roles	Rituals	Relationships
Irresponsibility	Don't be accountable	Sloth	Procrastination	Strained
Self-indulgence	If it feels good do it	Hedonist	Promiscuity	Egocentric
Interpersonal intrusiveness	If you want it take it	Bully	Condemnation	Intimidating
Social rule breaking	Rules were made to be broken	Rebel	Appropriation	Uncommitted

Table 4.2. Sample rules, roles, rituals, and relationships of a drug lifestyle

Behavioral characteristic	Rules	Roles	Rituals	Relationships
Pseudoresponsibility	Make it look good	Imposter	Simulation	Deceptive
Stress–coping imbalance	Escape from your problems	Quitter	Perplexity	Dependent
Interpersonal triviality	Don't get close	Know-It-All	Pomposity	Superficial
Social rule bending	Find a way around the rules	Swindler	Dishonesty	Manipulative

BEHAVIORAL CHARACTERISTICS OF A CRIMINAL LIFESTYLE

A criminal lifestyle is defined by the four behavioral styles of irresponsibility, self-indulgence, interpersonal intrusiveness, and social rule breaking.

Irresponsibility

Irresponsibility involves a lack of accountability and a general unwillingness to meet personal obligations to family, friends, employers, teachers, creditors, or even oneself. The behavioral style of irresponsibility follows the rule "don't concern yourself with being accountable." Roles assumed as part of this particular behavioral style include slothfulness, laziness, and unreliability. Procrastination, tardiness, and idleness are three major irresponsibility rituals. Additionally, the social relationships of people who operate on the basis of irresponsibility are strained and conflicted. The reason for this is that irresponsibility often leads to broken promises and unfulfilled expectations which become a source of frustration for those with whom one interacts.

Self-indulgence

Self-indulgence is an egocentric attempt to achieve immediate gratification. This may be expressed as drug use, gambling, or sexual promiscuity and can be a gateway to a drug, gambling, or sexual lifestyle. The cardinal rule of self-indulgence is to pursue activities that make one feel good irrespective of the negative long-term consequences. Hedonism, on the other hand, is the primary role adopted by people operating at the upper end of the self-indulgence continuum. Rituals that reflect self-indulgence include promiscuity, gambling, and drug use. Finally, the relationships self-indulgent people enter into are often self-serving and geared toward immediate gratification.

Interpersonal Intrusiveness

Interpersonal Intrusiveness connotes an incursion on the rights of others in which the privacy, dignity, or personal space of other people is violated. Murder, rape, and robbery are clear crimes of intrusion, but so are crimes like burglary and purse snatching. A rule that seems to characterize interpersonal intrusiveness holds that one has the right to commandeer other people's property with violence if necessary. The bully role is frequently visited by persons operating out of this particular behavioral style, and

the rituals that derive from the interpersonal intrusive style character-
istically involve putting others down or elevating oneself at the expense
of others. Finally, the social relationships that mark interpersonal
intrusiveness tend to be intimidating and exploitive.

Social Rule Breaking

Rules are required for social living, for even the criminal lifestyle
has rules. However, the rules of the criminal lifestyle often conflict with
the rules of the larger society. One rule governing the behavioral style
of social rule breaking states that since rules are made to be broken
one need not abide by the dictates of others. In actuality, the only rules
the individual breaches are conventional ones, since the rules of the
criminal subculture are normally followed (except in situations where
the apprehended criminal agrees to testify for the government in
exchange for a lighter sentence). The rebel role often guides social rule
breaking and a common ritual is appropriation whereby possessions,
ideas, or trust are stolen. The interpersonal relationships normally
found at the upper end of the social rule-breaking continuum lack
commitment, since commitments are viewed as conventional rules to
be broken.

Assessment: The Lifestyle Criminality Screening Form—Revised

The Lifestyle Criminality Screening Form (LCSF: Walters, White, &
Denney, 1991) is a 14-item chart audit form used to assess the four behavioral styles found in a criminal lifestyle. This instrument, recently revised
and reproduced in Appendix A, has been found to correlate with measures
of criminal history (Walters et al., 1991), antisocial personality (Walters
& Chlumsky, 1993), and future recidivism (Walters & Chlumsky, 1993;
Walters, Revella, & Baltrusaitis, 1990). A confirmatory factor analysis of
the LCSF revealed the superiority of a four-factor solution encompass-
ing the four standard LCSF scales (Irresponsibility, Self-indulgence,
Interpersonal Intrusiveness, Social Rule Breaking) over alternative one-
and two-factor solutions (Walters, 1997a). However, this study uncovered
even greater support for an alternate four-factor solution (antisocial identity, intrusiveness of the confining offense, family/interpersonal conflict,
poor school/work adjustment) identified in an earlier exploratory factor
analysis of the LCSF (Walters, 1995a). Given the relatively small number
of items present on each LCSF scale, contrasting the four standard scales
is of dubious value. A more defensible practice is to consider the total
LCSF score (range = 0 to 22). Research has consistently shown that scores
of 10 or higher on the LCSF are effective in identifying persons with solid

investment in a criminal lifestyle (Walters, 1995b; Walters & Chlumsky, 1993; Walters, White, & Denney, 1991).

BEHAVIORAL CHARACTERISTICS OF A DRUG LIFESTYLE

The behavioral styles used to define a drug lifestyle are irresponsibility/ pseudoresponsibility, stress-coping imbalance, interpersonal triviality, and social rule breaking/bending.

Irresponsibility/Pseudoresponsibility

Like the criminal lifestyle, the drug lifestyle is characterized by high levels of irresponsibility. However, the drug lifestyle is also marked by pseudo-responsibility in which the individual feigns responsibility—by maintaining employment, paying his or her bills, and staying out of prison—while failing to meet personal obligations to family members and close friends. Pseudoresponsibility is reflected in a man's decision to spend the evening with his drinking buddies rather than attend his child's birthday party or take his wife out for dinner on their anniversary. The cardinal rule of pseudoresponsibility is to put on appearances; a familiar role is that of the imposter, and common roles include simulation and imitation. Furthermore, the relationships observed in pseudoresponsibility are frequently marred by deception. It is often the case that as a drug lifestyle progresses, irresponsibility gradually replaces pseudoresponsibility.

Stress–Coping Imbalance

A reciprocal or bidirectional relationship has been found to exist between substance misuse and stress. Employing a three-wave panel design, Windle and Miller (1990) determined that higher levels of depression and problem drinking at Time 1 were followed by lower levels of problem drinking and depression, respectively, at Time 2. However, higher levels of depression and problem drinking at Time 2 correlated with higher levels of problem drinking and depression, respectively, at Time 3. One possible interpretation of these findings is that while drinking may initially reduce depression and vice versa, the alcohol–depression relationship changes with increased involvement in either behavior so that higher levels of depression eventually result in heavier drinking and higher levels in the use of alcohol lead to increased depression. This phenomenon, known in lifestyle theory circles as stress–coping imbalance, illustrates how a person's habitual manner of coping with stress (drug use) can actually contribute to the development of long-term stress even while it reduces short-term discomfort. Stress–coping imbalance is marked by pervasive rituals of perplexity and confusion, rules that exhort the person to run from his or her problems, roles that exonerate quitting, and relationships that place a premium on dependency.

Interpersonal Triviality

Humans are social animals whose survival depends on their ability to band together in groups. Whereas drug users also exhibit a social drive, they may shun intimate relationships because these relationships reduce the amount of time that can be spent in drug-related activities. Superficial interactions with other drug users, on the other hand, afford the individual human contact without removing him or her from the drug scene. Accordingly, a cardinal rule of interpersonal triviality is to avoid closeness and intimacy. A number of roles characterize the interpersonal triviality behavioral style, three of which—the drifter, social butterfly, and know-it-all—are described here. The drifter avoids commitment, the social butterfly flits from one superficial relationship to the next, and the know-it-all engages in vacuous conversations, often with other drug users, as a way of gaining social acceptance. Whether the topic is sports, politics, or drugs, the know-it-all performs the ritual of pomposity by acting as a resident expert on any and all subjects. Drug use rituals involving the procurement, preparation, and consumption of drugs also play a major role in interpersonal triviality since these rituals can serve as substitutes for deep, meaningful relationships.

Social Rule Breaking/Bending

The drug lifestyle is characterized by both social rule-breaking and social-rule bending behavior. Whereas social rule breaking concerns the violation of societal norms, customs, and edicts, social rule bending entails a subtle maneuvering around the rules. In a seeming paradox, this is the cardinal rule of social rule bending. Several different roles are enacted under the rubric of social rule bending, one of the more common being the swindler. This particular role calls for a number of dishonesty rituals, from lying, to cheating, to betraying, all in an effort to circumvent the rules. Quite obviously, the individual is prepared to break the rules in order to participate in a drug lifestyle. However, social rule bending is normally preferred because, if discovered, the person is less likely to experience severe punishment and be placed in situations, like jail, where he or she will have limited access to drugs. The relationships that support social rule bending are often manipulative and geared toward fulfilling the person's own "needs" regardless of how this may affect others.

Assessment: The Drug Lifestyle Screening Interview

The Drug Lifestyle Screening Interview (DLSI: Walters, 1994a) is a structured interview comprising four subscales designed to measure the four behavioral characteristics of a drug lifestyle: irresponsibility/pseudoresponsibility, stress-coping imbalance, interpersonal triviality, and social rule breaking/bending. Subscale scores range from 0 to 5 and scores on the DLSI cumulative index, a summation of the four subscales, range between 0 and 20. A cumulative index score of 10 or 11 is believed to reflect a drug-related preoccupation, while scores of 12 or higher indicate powerful involvement in, commitment to, and identification with a drug lifestyle (Walters, 1994a, 1995b). A two-year follow-up of 118 inmates, who were administered the DLSI prior to completing a prison-based residential drug intervention program, revealed a marginally significant predictive effect, with 21.7% of the high-scoring subjects (DLSI cumulative index $\geq$ 12) subsequently misusing alcohol or other drugs and 9.7% of the low-scoring subjects showing signs of substance misuse during the follow-up. However, the LCSF did an even better job of identifying subsequent relapse in this study: 27.3% of the inmates with LCSF scores of 10 or higher misused alcohol or other drugs during the follow-up compared to 4.4% of the inmates with LCSF scores below 10 (Walters, 1995b).

LIFESTYLES AND BEHAVIORAL CHARACTERISTICS: DICHOTOMY OR CONTINUUM?

In contrast to the dichotomous perspective on human behavior held by proponents of the disease and criminal justice models of drug–crime interaction, lifestyle theorists view drug use and crime as continua. Hence, rather than grouping people into dichotomized categories of behavior (e.g., diseased–non-diseased, addicted–non-addicted, criminal–non-criminal), the lifestyle model assumes that people function along a continuum of increasing drug or criminal involvement. This is also how the four behavioral styles are conceived. Each behavioral style is conceptualized as a separate continuum, although the different continua are frequently related. A person's position on a continuum is believed to be determined, in part, by the interacting influence of conditions, choices, and cognitions. These interactions hypothetically move the person up and down the continuum. Lifestyle theorists assert that these continua form a dynamic system rather than a static dichotomy. A lifestyle evolves as the individual begins spending significantly more time at the upper end of the continuum, which gradually alters the character of the continuum. Eventually, the continuum changes from one founded on behavioral initiation to one grounded in behavioral maintenance. This is the issue to which the present discussion now turns.

Although lifestyle theory holds firm to a continuous view of human behavior, there is evidence that behavioral patterns such as eating disorders (Laessle, Tuschl, Waadt, & Pirke, 1989), sexual preoccupation (Kafka & Prentky, 1992), and problem gambling (Corless & Dickerson, 1989) exhibit features of both a dichotomy and continuum. Hence, while eating-related concerns, sexual interest, and gambling seem to fall along a continuum of increasing involvement, there may be a point at which the continuum converts into a dichotomy. A similar pattern surfaced when the Psychological Inventory of Criminal Thinking Styles (PICTS) was administered to minimum-, medium-, and maximum-security inmates (Walters, 1995c). The outcome of this study, as portrayed in Figure 4.1, indicates that while the PICTS rose in conjunction with security level (which is known to correlate with criminal lifestyle involvement), the gap between medium- and maximum-security inmates is much greater than the difference between minimum- and medium-security inmates. These findings,

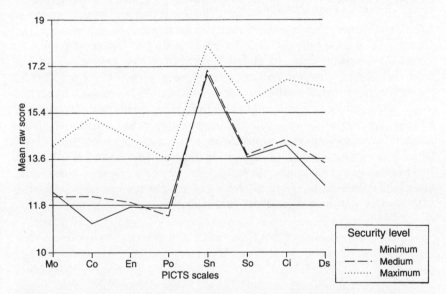

Figure 4.1. Comparison of minimum, medium, and maximum security inmates on the eight PICTS thinking style scales. (PICTS = Psychological Inventory of Criminal Thinking Styles; Mo = Mollification; Co = Cutoff; En = Entitlement; Po = Power orientation; Sn = Sentimentality; So = Superoptimism; Ci = Cognitive indolence; Ds = Discontinuity.) $N = 450$ male inmates (150 inmates per group)

coupled with the results of the previously mentioned eating disorder, sexual preoccupation, and problem gambling studies, insinuate that two continua may actually be operating. The first continuum is referred to by proponents of the lifestyle model as the open or linear continuum. People move freely along this continuum, but regular involvement at the upper end of this continuum leads to a transformation in which the open continuum becomes a closed or tubular continuum. It is in the closed continuum that the individual's behavior becomes compulsive and repetitive and where the focus shifts from one of initiation to one of maintenance.

The eight behavioral styles described in this chapter would appear to be prime targets for intervention. After all, our goal is to see substance-abusing offenders taking greater responsibility for their behavior, conforming to the norms and rules of society, and achieving higher levels of interpersonal intimacy. Unfortunately, the behavioral styles that define a drug or criminal lifestyle may be too complex and multifaceted to be of much use as guides to intervention. On the other hand, they can be extremely helpful in evaluating and documenting the success of an intervention over time. Instead of focusing on behavioral styles, therapists are advised to concentrate on the conditions, choices, and cognitions believed to play an instrumental role in the evolution of these behavioral styles. Since the three C's are vital to both the initiation and maintenance of lifestyle behavior, they are salient targets for intervention. Moreover, the three C's can be subdivided into basic skills that are more amenable to direct intervention than the global behavioral styles. Owing to the fact that conditions, choices, and cognitions vary widely there will be no general program that is effective for all clients. It is crucial, then, that one's interventions be tailored to the individual needs and strengths of the client, although there is sufficient patterning of behavior to allow dissemination of general guidelines for intervention. The next three chapters will investigate the three principal objectives of lifestyle intervention—arresting the lifestyle, teaching basic skills, encouraging resocialization—in an effort to demonstrate how a program of effective intervention can be initiated and maintained.

CHAPTER 5

Laying a Foundation for Change

The actions of the lifestyle therapist are guided by three primary objectives: arresting the lifestyle, developing basic skills, and encouraging resocialization. As many who have attempted to stop smoking or lose a few pounds can attest, a functional lifestyle provides little impetus for change. It is not until the lifestyle stops accomplishing its intended purpose that a person begins to contemplate the prospect of change. Accordingly, the first goal of lifestyle intervention is to arrest the lifestyle so that the individual can move on to more substantive issues. One of these more substantive issues is the development of basic skills, the second goal of lifestyle intervention. The third goal of intervention is to help clients identify a lifestyle incompatible with their continued misuse of substances or violation of societal rules—a procedure known as resocialization. Intervention can be divided into three phases, each of which corresponds to one of the primary goals of lifestyle intervention. Laying a foundation for change serves as the initial phase of intervention. It is during this phase that the goal of arresting the lifestyle assumes prominence. The middle phase—establishing and implementing vehicles of change—is designed to equip clients with basic social, coping, and life skills via a program of organized skills training. The late phase of intervention is designed to help clients cultivate a non-criminal/non-drug lifestyle incompatible with their continued involvement with drugs or crime. These divisions are referred to as phases rather than stages, in keeping with the holistic philosophy of lifestyle intervention. This chapter explores the foundational phase of lifestyle intervention and its primary objective, arresting the lifestyle.

MOTIVATION FOR CHANGE

Psychologists have traditionally viewed motivation as a stable, dispositional characteristic of the individual. The failure of planned change programs were accordingly attributed to disease, denial, resistance, or lack of will power on the part of the client. A very different perspective is offered by William Miller (1985) who argues that motivation is more unstable, situationally influenced, and interpersonally informed than has traditionally been assumed. Miller has transformed his views on motivation into an intervention known as motivational interviewing. This particular method entreats therapists to employ the following techniques in intervening with clients: accurate empathy, exploration of discrepancies (between personal goals and current behavior), avoidance of arguments, rolling with resistance, and supporting self-efficacy (Miller & Rollnick, 1991). These issues and techniques have been incorporated into the body of lifestyle intervention and play a particularly salient role in the early phases of intervention where arresting the lifestyle is the primary objective. The following discussion will be partitioned into three sections: initiating the arresting process, extending the arresting process, and looking beyond the arresting process.

INITIATING THE ARRESTING PROCESS

Change, it can be argued, begins with a crisis. This is because people whose lives are in good order and who are getting their wants and needs met are usually not motivated to change. It is only after a problem develops, or the lifestyle shows signs of falling short of personal goals and expectations, that people start questioning the lifestyle and considering the possibility of change. Borrowing from the discrepancy element of Miller's motivational interviewing approach, a crisis is defined as the point at which the client becomes aware of a discrepancy between his or her stated goals and current behavior. A crisis need not be negative or earth-shattering to effect a change in behavior. All that is required is that the situation, event, or thought be construed as personally relevant. Hence, marriage (Kandel & Raveis, 1989) and parenthood (Esbensen & Elliott, 1994) have been shown to portend decreasing levels of substance misuse in young adults, whereas an accumulation of daily hassles and risk factors may precede desistance from crime (Shover & Thompson, 1992). This underscores the perceptual nature of a crisis: i.e., one person's crisis is another's inconvenience. Lifestyle theory classifies crises by source (internal, external) and motive (approach-centered, avoidance-centered). An internally based crisis emanates from an endogenous source like disgust with one's behavior, as opposed to an externally based crisis wherein other people's reactions to one's behavior serve as the impetus for change. An approach-oriented crisis, on the other hand, is fueled by the desire to participate in activities other than the lifestyle, while an avoidance-oriented crisis is motivated by a desire to escape the pain and suffering engendered by one's involvement in a drug or criminal lifestyle.

Crossing source with motive yields four general categories of crisis: internal approach, external approach, internal avoidance, external avoidance (Walters, 1996b). Examples of each category are listed in Table 5.1. Lifestyle theory does not assume an equal distribution of cases across the four categories, only that these four categories represent the general types of crisis capable of eliciting an arresting response. It is conceivable that the crises that apparently support unassisted change and those that motivate formally assisted change differ in important ways. Approach-oriented crises and the accumulation of small avoidance-oriented crises (daily hassles), for instance, are reasonably common in persons who desist from substances like cocaine without benefit of formal intervention (Waldorf, Reinarman, & Murphy, 1991). Major avoidance-oriented crises, conversely, may be required in situations where the client has trouble desisting on his or her own and seeks the advice of a mental health professional or in situations where the client is deeply entrenched in a drug or criminal lifestyle. Be this as it may, there is still a common core from which all four categories of crisis spring. A crisis will arise only when people perceive that their behavior is preventing them from accomplishing a purpose to which they aspire or moving them closer to a purpose that they wish to avoid. Before a crisis can stimulate an initial change in behavior the individual must be willing to honestly evaluate his or her contributions to the problem. Procedures useful in defining, framing, and developing crises capable of facilitating the initial arresting of a drug or criminal lifestyle are described next.

Crises come and go, often without inspiring lasting change in a person's behavior. Short of creating a crisis, the therapist can augment the motivational process by identifying and exploring crises that occur naturally in a client's life. This can be accomplished by asking clients to construct

Table 5.1. Examples of crises divided by source and motive

	Source	
Motive	Internal	External
Approach-oriented	Desire for a legitimate career Aspirations for freedom	Getting married Parenthood
Avoidance-oriented	Disgust with life on the streets Sense of having "hit bottom"	Ultimatum from employer Shock of seeing crime partner killed

a list of people they have harmed, opportunities they have missed, relationships they have lost, and embarrassing situations they have encountered as a consequence of their involvement in a drug or criminal lifestyle. The therapist can then follow this up by having the client identify the common element in each of these negative situations (the answer being the client). Imagery techniques and interventions that highlight the discrepancies between a person's behavior and stated goals are additional ways of developing a crisis. Maximum development of a crisis, however, requires the formation of an introspective attitude, no small task in someone with a strong external orientation. Introspection entails a willingness to look within oneself and construct a thorough inventory of one's thoughts and actions rather than blame outside circumstances. This is similar to how the moral inventory is used in twelve-step programs. Techniques capable of inspiring an introspective attitude in clients include yoga or meditation, personal diaries or journals, and self-monitoring. Self-monitoring is a behavioral technique in which clients observe and chart their thoughts and actions. By focusing the client's attention on his or her thinking and behavior the therapist establishes a framework for introspection, which can then be used to arrest a drug or criminal lifestyle.

EXTENDING THE ARRESTING PROCESS

The ability of crises to arrest a lifestyle varies widely, but there are few crises that suspend lifestyle patterns of behavior indefinitely. It is for this very reason that the initial arresting process must be extended and maintained. One way this may be accomplished is through creation of a robust client–therapist relationship. This relationship may, in fact, encourage a reaction in clients similar to the placebo effect described in the psychopharmacology literature in which people respond to an inert substance they are told is a psychoactive drug. Anticipation of a positive outcome from one's interaction with a psychotherapist can create an initial positive expectancy that facilitates growth of an alliance between the therapist and client. Lifestyle therapists refer to this as the shaman effect, a term derived from both the pharmacological placebo effect and the historical role of shamanistic healers in hunting and gathering societies (Walters, 1997b). Shamans are magico-religious practitioners who attempt to "heal" the members of their tribe or community by entering into an altered state of consciousness (understanding the problem), taking a mythical journey (confronting the problem), and bringing the client back into harmony with the larger community (overcoming the problem). Although the techniques may differ, the goals of shamanistic healers and psychotherapists are similar. It has even been argued that the therapist and relationship factors known to correlate with positive therapeutic outcome are reflective of psychotherapy's shamanistic roots (Walters, 1997b). Lifestyle therapists consequently seek to extend and maintain the arresting process by creating a shaman effect, the five key elements of which are sensitivity, ritual, metaphor, dialectics, and the attribution triad.

Sensitivity

For the shaman effect to take root the client must believe that the therapist understands his or her inner world. This can be accomplished with the aid of several different techniques, accurate empathy, prediction, and interpretation being three of the more common vehicles used to demonstrate sensitivity. All major schools of psychotherapy have at least one vehicle capable of accessing a client's internal frame of reference. The degree to which a therapist is able to reflect sensitivity may predict the future success of intervention by virtue of its ability to contribute to the evolution of a shaman effect. The extent to which meaning is relational, gaining and projecting an accurate understanding of a client's inner world, whether through interpretation, empathy, or prediction, provides the client with assurance that he or she might also eventually be in a position to comprehend what is presently a very confusing world (Kirmayer, 1993).

Ritual

Rituals are one of the four R's that define a lifestyle. However, rituals can also be growth-enhancing and empowering. Criteria used to discriminate between constructive and destructive rituals include: (1) whether the ritual promotes self-assurance or self-doubt; (2) whether the ritual fosters social connectiveness or social isolation; (3) whether the ritual opens the door to new opportunities or closes the door on current experience. Psychotherapy, in fact, is a kind of ritual. The client meets with the same therapist, often in the same office, on the same day, at the same time. The course of a session also assumes features of a ritual as issues are broached, goals formulated, and closure achieved, all within a single 50-minute session. It is essential, however, that therapeutic rituals be used to provide clients with reassurance and a sense of rational control over their lives rather than establishing a new lifestyle of rigid routines and dogmatic beliefs.

Metaphor

Rhetoric and the way in which a therapist enforces the melodic requirements of speech can sometimes transform perceptions, thoughts, and feelings in clients (Frank & Frank, 1991). Metaphors not only rely on the melodic requirements of speech but also concretize abstract concepts into tangible symbols which can be manipulated and explored in therapy sessions with less resistance and more understanding than is typically achieved in sessions that focus on the abstract concepts themselves (McMullen, 1989). Metaphors can solidify the therapeutic alliance by bringing the therapist and client closer together by way of a shared private language (Cohen, 1979). The resulting relationship plays a major role in boosting a client's confidence in his or her own ability to overcome personal problems, skill deficits, and environmental impediments.

Dialectics

Myths play an integral role in the shaman effect but must be reinforced with empirical, teleological, and epistemological constructs to be life-affirming. Empirical constructs are accessed through sensitivity and ritual, epistemological constructs through metaphor, and teleological constructs through dialectics. The dialectic method necessitates contrasting a thesis (idea) with its antithesis (counter-idea) to create a synthesis (new idea). The shaman effect is facilitated by contrasting dysfunctional myths with their respective counter-myths. The end result is a synthesis that is frequently more sophisticated and adaptable than either of the two myths from whence it sprang (Feinstein & Krippner, 1988).

Attribution Triad

The overall objective of the shaman effect is to encourage clients to believe in themselves and their ability to manage the problems of everyday living. Attributions are beliefs about the causes of behavior (Weiner, 1974). Self-attributions are at the heart of the shaman effect since attributions of non-accountability, hopelessness, and self-doubt fail to establish the proper mental attitude for change. The attribution triad can be viewed as a set of thoughts, beliefs, and attributions potentially capable of transforming the irresponsibility, fatalism, and powerlessness of a drug or criminal lifestyle into responsibility, hope, and empowerment. This is accomplished by reinforcing the three beliefs that form the attribution triad. These three beliefs include a belief in the necessity of change, a belief in the possibility of change, and a belief in one's ability to effect change.

The first branch of the attribution triad holds that a person must aver a belief in the necessity of change before change can occur. This means that clients must appreciate the urgency and eventuality of change and be willing to make the necessary changes in their thinking and behavior.

Although easier said than done, the degree to which a person internalizes these beliefs is a good indicator of the power the shaman effect has to arrest a drug or criminal lifestyle. Research shows that substance abusers (Haines & Ayliffe, 1991) and criminal offenders (Ross & Fabiano, 1985) have an external locus of control and that with intervention such individuals often become more internally oriented (Oswald, Walker, Krajewski, & Reilly, 1994). One goal of early stage intervention, then, is to encourage clients to take responsibility for their lives and discuss with them the consequences of continuing to avoid their responsibilities.

The second branch of the attribution triad reflects a belief in the possibility of change. Some clients believe that change is necessary but have little faith in other people's, let alone their own, ability to change. Making arrangements for clients to meet with members of the community who have successfully abandoned a drug or criminal lifestyle can help dispel the unsubstantiated myth that because tigers do not change their stripes nor leopards their spots, people do not change their behavior. Use of the dialectic method (Krippner, 1986), and various rational-behavioral exercises designed to illustrate how one's feelings change as a consequence of alterations in thinking (Ellis, 1970), can also lay claim to instilling a belief in the possibility of change. Perhaps the most important contribution made by a belief in the possibility of change is that it furnishes the client with hope that his or her life circumstances can change.

The final branch of the attribution triad professes a belief in the ability to effect change. Acceptance of this belief signals confidence in one's ability to manage the temptations and frustrations that may lead to relapse. Bailey, Hser, Hsieh, and Anglin (1994) followed a group of 354 narcotic-dependent subjects for 24 years and determined that 59 (16.7%) could be classified as "winners": so classified because they gave no indication of narcotic or serious drug use and had not been involved in criminal activity in the last 36 months. Eighty-five percent of the "winners" expressed "complete confidence" in their ability to refrain from narcotic usage over the next year compared to 18% of subjects contemporaneously involved with drugs or currently incarcerated. Whether confidence causes behavior or behavior causes confidence cannot be determined from the results of this study since the self-reports were retrospective rather than prospective. Nonetheless, the empowerment that results from internalizing the belief in one's ability to effect change is a major goal of lifestyle intervention.

Belief in the ability to effect change is both general and specific. The general features of this belief affirm confidence in one's ability to impact on the environment through self-determination. Effectance motivation is another term commonly used to describe this process (White, 1959). Confidence in one's ability to manage specific situations, such as those in which drugs are involved or crimes committed, comes under the heading of self-efficacy (Bandura, 1977). Both general and specific confidence impact on behavior, but there is no substitute for successful performance of a skill when it comes to inculcating effectance motivation and self-efficacy. The more the client experiences success the more he or she is likely to feel confident in his or her abilities and skills. Hence, the skill-building techniques described in the next chapter are of major consequence in developing and reinforcing a client's belief in his or her ability to effect change. Learning the skill, being able to practice it in role play situations, receiving feedback, and successfully applying the skill in real-life situations is consequently a major source of self-confidence.

LOOKING BEYOND THE ARRESTING PROCESS

When moving beyond the foundational phase of intervention it may be helpful to consider Prochaska and DiClemente's (1992) stages-of-change model. As was made clear in the opening section of this chapter, motivation, rather than being a stable person characteristic, is actually a process that changes over time. Consequently, the therapist must take advantage of opportunities for intervention and match these interventions with the prevailing motivational state of the client. This can be accomplished by taking note of Prochaska and DiClemente's five stages of change. The first stage, precontemplation, is characterized by minimal motivation for change because the individual sees no problem with his or her behavior. This is followed by contemplation in which the client experiences negative consequences but is still not sure whether he or she wants to actively pursue change. The primary emotion displayed during this stage is ambivalence. The third stage in the Prochaska and DiClemente model is preparation. This is marked by a growing commitment to change. The fourth or action stage is predicated on active modification of problematic thoughts, feelings, and actions. The fifth stage, referred to by Prochaska and DiClemente as maintenance, is designed to consolidate gains accrued in earlier stages and avoid relapse. It is reasoned that clients continue to cycle through the stages until they either abandon the lifestyle or re-enter the precontemplation stage (Miller & Rollnick, 1991). The entire system, along with its entrance and exit points, is depicted in Figure 5.1.

Given the nature of motivation and change the therapist can help his or her cause by becoming sensitive to the stage of change at which the client is currently functioning. Once the proper stage has been identified the therapist can match the client to an appropriate intervention strategy since some interventions are better suited to certain stages than others (DiClemente, Prochaska, Fairhurst, Velicer, Velasquez, & Rossi,

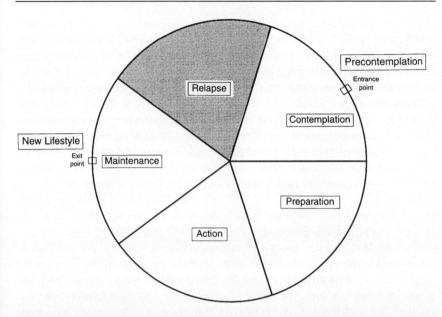

Figure 5.1 Prochaska and DiClemente's stages-of-change model. (Adapted from Miller, W. R., & Rollnick, S., 1991.)

1991). For clients in a state of precontemplation the therapist is advised to consider interventions that focus on the development of crises and highlight the discrepancies that exist between the client's goals and behavior. Therapists working with clients who are in a contemplative mood might want to consider the emotional relief that occurs with the shaman effect and then use imagery to foster a sense of disgust with prior and current drug or criminal involvement. The preparation stage lends itself best to interventions such as values clarification and the first two branches (belief in the necessity of change, belief in the possibility of change) of the attribution triad. For clients currently falling into the action stage skills training and interventions designed to increase self-efficacy and effectance motivation—particularly those that call for performance of a learned skill—may yield the best results. Finally, clients operating out of the maintenance stage are most receptive to interventions that emphasize self-reinforcement, social support, and the resocialization process. Although the match is not perfect, the interventions viewed as appropriate for the different stages of change frequently correspond to the three phases of intervention: i.e., first three stages relate to the foundational phase, the action stage to the vehicle phase, and the maintenance stage to the reinforcing lifestyle phase.

Contrary to the theoretical formulations and empirical studies of Jessor and Jessor (1977), White and Labouvie (1994) found evidence in a longitudinal investigation of male and female youth that deviance is not always undifferentiated and that some individuals specialize in either substance abuse or delinquency. Nevertheless, the professionals and paraprofessionals for whom this book was written are tasked with the responsibility of working with clients whose involvements, commitments, and identifications often involve both drugs and crime. For this reason, both lifestyles often need to be addressed. The second phase of lifestyle intervention will be the focus of discussion in the next chapter, followed by a review of the third and final phase of intervention in Chapter 7. For economy's sake, interventions that are effective with both substance abuse and crime are emphasized in this book. However, there are substance-abusing offenders whose greatest involvement is with substances and whose criminality is largely a consequence of their substance misuse and vice versa, and these individual variations need to be taken into account in constructing a plan of intervention for clients. There is no blueprint for intervention, only general guidelines and suggestions. As was pointed out in the previous section, the therapeutic alliance may be a more powerful predictor of long-term outcome than specific intervention strategies and tactics. As was noted in the present section, the therapist would be well advised to encourage clients to eventually exit the recovery process, as represented by the stages of change; if clients continually cycle through these stages, this invites relapse. The reader should keep these issues in mind as we move beyond the arresting process into a discussion of the second and third phases of lifestyle intervention.

CHAPTER 6

Identifying Vehicles for Change

There are many reasons for the surfeit of skill deficits found in people who misuse substances and commit serious crime. For some such individuals, the skill deficit is a cause of their drug and criminal involvement. For others, the skill deficit is a consequence of their commitment to a drug or criminal lifestyle since such commitment limits people's opportunities for new skill development. For still others, the skill deficit and drug/criminal involvement evolved bidirectionally or epiphenomenally. Regardless of how the skill deficit–drug/crime nexus is conceived, there is little doubt that a relationship does, in fact, exist between these variables. With this in mind, we turn our attention to the second goal of lifestyle intervention, that of building skills that have either atrophied through years of disuse or were never learned in the first place. The vehicles referred to in the title of this chapter are the tools by which therapists instruct clients in basic skills. There are many more tools than could possibly be addressed in a chapter of this size, and it was necessary to pare down the number of vehicles considered. The overriding criterion for inclusion of a vehicle was its perceived capacity to stimulate skill development with respect to one of the three C's of lifestyle theory: conditions, choices, and cognitions. More global strategies and vehicles will be covered in the final chapter of this book.

CONDITION-BASED VEHICLES

There are two general categories of condition: historical–developmental conditions and current–contextual conditions. Historical–developmental conditions are person, situation, and interactive variables that have helped shape a person's decisions and behavior, but, because they are no longer in effect, do not lend themselves to intervention. Current–contextual conditions, on the other hand, can be altered because they are ongoing conditional influences, even if they have their roots in historical–developmental processes. Research indicates that current–contextual conditions like negative mood states, environmental cues, drug availability, and interpersonal pressure figure prominently in substance abusers' explanations for relapse (Bradley, Phillips, Green, & Gossop, 1989; Litman, Stapleton, Oppenheim, Peleg, & Jackson, 1983; Marlatt & Gordon, 1985). Current-contextual conditions may also predict recidivism in criminal populations (Ross & Fabiano, 1985). The Estimated Self-efficacy in Avoiding Drugs and Estimated Self-efficacy in Avoiding Crime forms reproduced in Appendices C and D of this text assess five current–contextual conditions with high relapse potential (i.e., negative affect, positive affect, cues, availability, interpersonal influence). Intervention may be called for when the mean score of one of these five sections dips below the client's total scale mean. Specific vehicles designed to improve a person's capacity to cope with salient current–contextual conditions are described next. First, however, it is important to understand that the Estimated Self-efficacy in Avoiding Drugs and Crime measures, in addition to assessing specific current–contextual conditions, provide information on a client's general confidence in his or her ability to cope with drug- and crime-related situations (total score of 76–80 = high degree of confidence, if not overconfidence; 66–75 = realistic level of confidence; 56–65 = marginal confidence; <56 = minimal confidence).

Affect Regulation

Positive as well as negative affect can precipitate a relapse. In a 30-month follow-up of 73 male alcohol-abusing Veterans Administration outpatients, McKay, Maisto, and O'Farrell (1996) discerned that positive affect ("feeling good") was more vital than negative affect ("feeling down") in predicting relapse during the first three months of a 30-month follow-up, but that negative affect became a more potent predictor of relapse near the end of the follow-up period. This same study showed that anxious affect ("feeling uptight") was a robust predictor of relapse at all six follow-ups (3 months, 6 months, 12 months, 18 months, 24 months, and 30 months). In an earlier study conducted by some of these same investigators, a group of adolescents were found to attribute their use of substances to the positive features of drug use (pleasant emotions, pleasant times with others) rather than various negative factors (unpleasant emotions, conflict with others). However, negative factors seemed to predominate in subjects more heavily involved with substances (McKay, Murphy, McGuire, Rivinus, & Maisto, 1992). These outcomes suggest that positive affect may initially motivate substance use and accordingly be an early high-risk condition for relapse, but that negative affect tends to become increasingly more important at higher levels of usage and later in the recovery process. Negative affect, in the form of depression, boredom, and frustration, may also portend recidivism in criminal populations (Cusson & Pinsonneault, 1986).

Positive, negative, and anxious affect all appear to play a role in relapse and recidivism, although the role may vary with the stage of recovery demonstrated by the individual. During the early stages of recovery the focus should probably be on positive affect. One feature of positive affect that might reasonably be tagged for intervention is the desire to have a good time with former lifestyle associates. Clients must understand that it is not in their best interests to associate with people still involved with drugs and crime. Decision-making and assertiveness training can help reduce the odds of a client yielding to the desire to associate with former lifestyle cohorts. Assertiveness training, in which clients are taught to assert themselves and stand up for their rights, has been shown to be effective with substance-abusing clients (Ingram & Salzberg, 1990). Although teaching offenders to assert themselves may seem unnecessary and redundant, assertiveness skills can be helpful in altering the aggressive, interpersonally intrusive styles commonly observed in criminal populations. Overconfidence is a second manifestation of positive affect with clear implications for intervention. The therapist can help prevent overconfidence by strengthening the resolve of clients to critically appraise information presented to them through the media (Ross & Fabiano, 1985). By learning to evaluate, assess, and resist advertising pressure, as well as other forms of interpersonal influence, clients augment their capacity to think critically. This, in turn, reduces their chances of falling victim to overconfidence.

Negative affect, such as depression and anger, can trigger relapse and recidivism by instilling a sense of hopelessness and futility in clients. There is some indication that negative affect's role in relapse may grow over the course of the post-release period. With time, clients may lose jobs and relationships, two of the primary external precipitants of negative affect. People who are not prepared to handle these negative external events are at increased risk for relapse as they try to find comfort, security, and support. Emotions management is one vehicle that can be used to intervene with negative affect. Although most commonly found in interventions for anger (Lochman, 1992), emotions management can also be helpful in combatting depression, frustration, and boredom. The first step in using emotions management is to outline the nature of emotion and its relationship to thinking and behavior for clients. The next step is to provide training in self-control techniques like progressive muscular relaxation. The third step is to instruct clients in coping self-talk designed to manage negative affect. This is followed by efforts to encourage clients to share their feelings in an effort to relieve pressure, solicit support, and obtain feedback. The final step in the process is to have clients construct a diary specific to the emotion that has been targeted (an anger diary for anger, a depression diary for depression) within which feelings, stimulus conditions, and associated thoughts are charted, followed, and discussed with the therapist in order to apply the emotions management technique to real-life situations.

The first step in coping with anxious affect is to thoroughly evaluate the conditions under which anxiety is manifest. The Lifestyle Stress Test (see Appendix E) is a measure specifically designed for this purpose. With an inventory of 20 situations, the Lifestyle Stress Test provides a total score and two subscale scores—personal sources of stress (odd numbered items) and interpersonal sources of stress (even numbered items)—for two time frames (the month during which the respondent was most heavily involved with drugs and crime and the preceding 30 days). The total score affords an overall estimate of the respondent's stress level: <15, minimal stress; 15–24 moderately low stress; 25–34, moderately high stress; ⩾35, high stress. Whereas the total score reflects the client's general stress level, the subscales may prove more fruitful when it comes to selecting a specific course of intervention. If the "personal sources of stress" score significantly exceeds the "interpersonal sources of stress" score then interventions like relaxation, yoga, time management, and rational restructuring are indicated. Conversely, if "interpersonal sources of stress" predominate then the appropriate intervention would be something along the lines of assertiveness or social-communication skills training. Regardless of whether the Lifestyle Stress Test or an alternative measure is employed, the client needs to understand that the goal in managing his or her stress is to harness energy he or she is currently wasting on non-productive activity and channel it into positive and life-affirming pursuits.

Cue Control

Cues are stimulus conditions capable of eliciting a response that is often perceived by the individual as craving. These cues can either be environmental (exteroceptive cues) or internal (interoceptive cues). Examples of environmental cues include the teller counter for someone who has formed a lifestyle around bank robbery and the smell of burnt sulfur emanating from a lighted match for someone who has converted the intravenous use of drugs into a lifestyle. Interoceptive cues are the behaviors (rituals), thoughts (positive outcome expectancies), and feelings (anger) that elicit a desire to engage in crime or drug use. Exteroceptive cues associated with a simulated bar/lounge were found to elicit a desire for alcohol in a group of problem drinkers regardless of whether they consumed alcohol or an alcohol-like placebo (McCusker & Brown, 1990). Exteroceptive cues also have a demonstrated ability to stimulate the urge to use heroin (Childress, McLellan, & O'Brien, 1986) and cocaine (Childress, McLellan, Ehrman, & O'Brien, 1987) in currently abstinent heroin and cocaine abusers. Interoceptive cues are likewise capable of producing craving in those who habitually ingest alcohol (Bigelow, Griffiths, & Liebson, 1977), amphetamines (Chait, Uhlenhuth, & Johanson, 1986), and morphine (Preston, Bigelow, Bickel, & Liebson, 1987). Although cues have received much less attention in studies on crime, recidivism in sex offenders has been shown to correlate with arousal to deviant sexual stimuli subsequent to a counter-conditioning intervention (Quinsey & Marshall, 1983).

The twelve-step philosophy of avoiding "people, places, and things" associated with one's past involvement with drugs and crime can be an excellent starting point for interventions designed to curb the craving for drugs. After identifying the people, places, and things (including rituals, thoughts, and feelings) capable of invoking the urge to use drugs or commit crime, the client selects one of two general coping strategies. The simplest strategy is to avoid the people, places, and things that elicit a craving response, whether this means staying out of banks or avoiding lighted matches. Because cue avoidance is not always possible, it may be necessary to implement a procedure known as cue exposure. This entails presenting a stimulus condition or cue to clients while simultaneously preventing them from completing the drug or criminal response. If there is any validity to classical conditioning then arousal should extinguish with repeated unreinforced exposure to the cue. There is circumscribed support for the use of cue exposure with alcohol (Drummond & Glautier, 1994) and cocaine (O'Brien, Childress, McLellan, & Ehrman, 1990) and a case report of a young male fire setter who benefited from repeatedly lighting matches until he tired of the activity (Daniel, 1987). The lifestyle model, in addition to presenting the cue, instructs and guides the client in the generation of a coping response capable of reducing the uncomfortable sensations (withdrawal-like symptomatology) inspired by the cue. The advantage of this coping skills version of the cue exposure paradigm is that it provides clients with a general skill that can be used to manage uncomfortable feelings elicited by cues other than the ones upon which training was based.

Access Reduction

The availability of heroin has been cited as vital to both initial opiate usage (Simpson & Marsh, 1986) and later relapse (Meyer & Mirin, 1979). Reducing opportunities for crime, in turn, has been shown to be effective in attenuating the crime rates of communities that have implemented such target-hardening procedures as enhanced street lighting, reduced access to residences, and neighborhood watch programs (MacDonald & Gifford, 1989). The first step in reducing drug availability and criminal opportunities is to have clients specify how they might limit their access to drugs and crime. A common access reduction technique is to have a close friend or family member initially manage one's finances since ready access to cash is a path that can lead one back into a drug lifestyle. Access to future criminality can be reduced by encouraging offenders to avoid carrying firearms based on the realization that possession of a weapon by a felon is an infraction punishable by law. The mere act of carrying a weapon puts the person in a position of using the weapon, for without it he or she would need to consider other alternatives in confronting the problems of everyday living. Geographic relocation is a strategy that has been found effective in reducing future opportunities for drug abuse (Maddux & Desmond, 1982) and crime (Cusson & Pinsonneault, 1986). As a stand-alone procedure, however, geographic location will do little to alleviate the problems of drug abuse and crime. Relocation simply makes it easier for a person with commitment to change to avoid certain opportunities for drug use and crime.

Interpersonal Change

Interpersonal influence encompasses a number of overt and subtle social factors that seem to support a drug or criminal lifestyle. In reviewing the circumstances leading up to criminal assault, Felson, Ribner, and Siegel (1984) determined that more blows were struck when bystanders, often family members and friends, encouraged violence whereas fewer blows were struck when bystanders served as mediators. Similarly, program participants who re-establish ties with drug-using associates experience a heightened rate of relapse upon release (Marlatt & Gordon, 1980). Finding a new group of friends therefore qualifies as a potent vehicle for managing problems stemming from interpersonal forms of negative influence. Self-remitting alcohol abusers, when asked about their reasons for desisting from an alcohol-based lifestyle, mentioned development of a new network of friends as a core motive in their decision to exit the lifestyle (Tuchfeld, 1981). Shover (1983) reports that establishment of a new intimate relationship or re-establishment of an old intimate relationships boded well for lasting change in later stage property offenders. There is also the suggestion that access reduction techniques (relocation) and interpersonal change strategies (new social network) may supplement one another since relocating often entails finding a new set of friends. However, the new friends will be very much like the old friends unless the relocation is accompanied by an equally powerful commitment to change. Since it is not always possible to avoid old drug and criminal associates, additional skill development in the form of social-communication and assertiveness skills training may be required.

A relatively high rate of interpersonal problem-solving deficits has been documented in substance-abusing (Beatty, Katzung, Moreland, & Nixon, 1995) and delinquent (Campanella, 1990) populations. There is even evidence that ingestion of a substance like alcohol may precipitate aggressive behavior by interfering with a person's ability to solve problems (Pihl & Peterson, 1995). The problem-solving approach, which has been found efficacious in reducing relapse (Joe, Brown, & Simpson, 1995) and recidivism (Larson, 1992), follows a basic five-step procedure (see Figure 6.1). The first step is to define the problem in terms that are clear, precise, and behavioral. Once the problem has been defined, the next step is to generate as many different alternative solutions to the problem as possible. Instead of evaluating alternatives as they are generated, a more

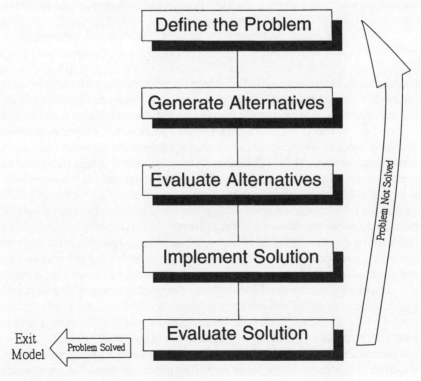

Figure 6.1 The problem-solving model.

productive strategy is to list all possible solutions regardless of how untenable they may at first appear. The third step of the interpersonal problem-solving approach is to evaluate the advantages (pros) and disadvantages (cons) of each generated alternative. Once this has been accomplished the individual selects one or more of the alternatives and puts them into action. After a period of time the solution is evaluated to determine if the problem has, in fact, been solved. If the problem has been solved then the problem-solving sequence is terminated. In the event the problem is not solved, the client should be encouraged to repeat the process, starting with the first step, problem definition. This is because the single most important reason for failure is often a poorly or improperly defined problem. The problem-solving skill affords clients a general skill that can be employed across a wide range of different situations.

Fear Management

Lifestyle theory considers person and situation variables critical in establishing the conditional parameters of a person's life. Even greater emphasis, however, is placed on the interaction of individual person and situation variables. The first four current–contextual conditions described in this section—affective responses, cues, availability, and interpersonal influence—reflect different categories of person × situation interaction. Existential fear, and its progenitors, survival strain and primal fear, encompasses a person (survival instinct) by situation (constantly changing environment) interaction which is at once historical–developmental and current–contextual. In this way, the existential fear lineage is the primordial person × situation interaction. There are two basic motives that prompt entrance into a lifestyle. First, there is escape from the feared object and second, there is the search for a palliative. The first response is referred to as "fleeing from fear" and the second as "chasing the phantom." Lifestyle theory contends that existential fear is inescapable because it is grounded in the conditions of a person's life. This does not seem to deter people, however, from using the lifestyle to escape from fear. The escape, even though it is illusory, momentarily reduces, but does not eliminate, the fear. The lifestyle becomes a palliative for the remaining fear through its ability to link early surface ("drugs will make me popular and provide me with a good feeling") and deep ("drugs will eliminate all of my insecurities and self-doubt") expectancies. The palliative function of a lifestyle is just as illusory as the escape function, however, because it fails to address the underlying existential fear.

Existential fear, because it is a unique expression of a person's current life situation, must first be assessed. The personalization of existential fear occurs through its interaction with other life conditions. Three early life experiences play a particularly salient role in this process: these experiences being referred to as attachment, control, and self-image. Difficulties involving any one of these experiences help transform and mold existential fear around specific themes. People with problems of attachment, for instance, tend to exhibit fears of intimacy and rejection, whereas those with issues centering on control are more apt to express power- or control-related concerns. Clients who struggle with the self-image life task, on the other hand, often fear a loss of identity or become preoccupied with themes of success and failure. The Fear Checklist (see Appendix F) provides a means by which the individual contributions of attachment (bonding column), control (orientation column), and self-image (identity column) to a person's experience of existential fear can be evaluated. Therapists can get an even better picture of a client's existential fear by having him or her draw the fear with colored pens or pencils. By projecting their fear onto paper clients can achieve greater distance, understanding, and mastery over these ordinarily perplexing feelings. Fear management techniques such as relaxation training and desensitization can also help keep existential fear in check, as can an analysis of the deep and surface expectancies that contribute to the development of a client's phantom. Frequently, when people begin to realize that their chase is futile they begin to question the ability of a lifestyle to accomplish its intended purpose.

CHOICE-BASED VEHICLES

The goal of choice-based vehicles is to provide clients with skills that allow them to make choices which, from a utilitarian point of view, are capable of maximizing benefits and minimizing costs. This can be accomplished by increasing options and improving decision-making competence. The first set of strategies are referred to as option expansion techniques, whereas the second set are known as competence enhancement techniques.

Option Expansion

There are several ways a person can increase his or her options in life. As the reader may recall, the objective of the second stage of interpersonal problem solving is to generate as many different alternative solutions as possible. People who can suspend judgement long enough to entertain a range of options are in a better position to solve a problem than people who jump to conclusions after generating only one or two alternatives. Creativity and innovation are therefore necessary prerequisites for effective problem solving and option expansion. Clients can realize these goals by strengthening their divergent or lateral thinking skills. In contrast to convergent or vertical thinking, where an optimal solution is sought, lateral thinking focuses on assembling as many different alternative solutions as possible (de Bono, 1977). Given the cognitive rigidity and weak creativity observed in those who abuse substances (Ryan & Butters, 1983) and habitually commit crime (Miller, 1988), lateral skills training would seem advisable in a large majority of cases. To determine whether a specific client might benefit from such training the clinician may want to consider administering the Multiple Options Analysis (see Appendix G). Clients who generate fewer than an average of five options per problem should be considered in need of lateral thinking skills training. A procedure potentially useful in encouraging lateral thinking skill development is to present a cartoon to clients for which they must supply their own caption. Variations on this theme include having clients compose a story from lines extracted from a magazine or newspaper article or having clients construct a larger object from a series of seemingly unrelated smaller objects. Once these tasks have been performed the therapist can ask the client to generate a new series of captions, stories, and constructions to the same cartoons, articles, and objects.

Another way clients can expand their options is through social skill development. A socially skilled individual has many more options than someone who lacks social skills, and research indicates that social competence is particularly poor in situations where drug abuse and antisociality thrive (Luthar, Glick, Zigler, & Rounsaville, 1993). The socially skilled individual can talk and negotiate his or her way out of, around, or through a disagreement because of the social skills at his or her disposal. The socially unskilled person's response, on the other hand, is limited by his or her lack of skills. Social-communication skill deficits have been recorded in both substance abusers (Hover & Gaffney, 1991) and criminal offenders (Oyserman & Saltz, 1993) thereby making it imperative that therapists at least consider social skills in their work with substance-abusing criminal offenders. Interventions designed to ameliorate social skill deficits follow a basic four-step procedure. Initially, the social skill deficit is identified and the client taught to recognize and decipher relevant verbal and non-verbal social cues. Clips from television shows with the sound turned off can be used to demonstrate how nonverbal cues facilitate our comprehension of social situations. After the segment has been shown, clients should be asked for their analysis and a review of the social cues upon which they based their conclusions. The segment can then be re-shown, this time with the sound turned up, to illustrate how verbal cues contribute additional information to our understanding of social situations. The second step in teaching social skills is to partition the social skill (e.g., asking a stranger for directions) into its component subskills (e.g., eye contact, verbal tone, body posture, interpersonal distance, listening, verbal expression) and review each component with clients. The third step is to arrange for clients to practice the skill and its components in role play situations with ample amounts of feedback and reinforcement. This is then followed by a generalization phase in which the client is encouraged to apply the skill in real-life situations.

Life skills, such as opening a bank account or purchasing a car, can also be imparted to clients in the name of option expansion. Life skills training, in fact, is a major component of Oregon's Cornerstone therapeutic community program for substance-abusing criminal offenders. Participants who complete this program, which emphasizes money management, nutrition, and job skill training, typically display moderately positive outcomes following release (Field, 1992). The life skills training process normally begins with a review of the client's level of comfort with and perceived competence in such varied skills as personal hygiene, clothing maintenance, food preparation, money management, job procurement, leisure time activities, and dating. This is followed by training in those areas for which the client feels less than fully confident and/or competent. The life skills training process comprises basic instruction, role playing, and generalization to real-life situations in consultation with the therapist. Life skills training can be instrumental in easing a client's transition back into the community, but can be just as effective if used on an outpatient basis. Occupational and educational skills are also capable of expanding a person's options in life, but often require the use of professionals whose expertise is in the educational and occupational areas rather than in the mental health or addictions fields.

Competence Enhancement

Expanded options are worthless if the client is not in a position to effectively evaluate these options and select an optimal solution. Clients must consequently be taught the proper manner of evaluating and selecting options. Cost–benefit analysis is one technique that can be of assistance in enhancing decision-making competence. Someone conducting a cost–benefit analysis begins by listing the perceived costs (negative aspects) and benefits (positive aspects) of each option under consideration. These anticipated outcomes are then weighed or ordered by the individual using a generalized strategy (e.g., the advantages of A are stronger than the advantages of B; the disadvantages of C are greater than the disadvantages of D) or more specific evaluation (e.g., advantage #1 for A is worth +14 points, advantage #2 for A is worth +4 points; disadvantage

#1 for B is worth −6 points, disadvantage #2 for B is worth −19 points). The client then tallies the respective costs and benefits of each option and calculates an option's total perceived utility (benefit − cost). The total perceived utilities of the different options are then compared and the one with the highest perceived utility selected. As with the problem-solving approach, a follow-up is conducted in an effort to evaluate the success of the selected option. Few people regularly utilize a formal cost–benefit analysis in their everyday decisions. Nevertheless, by raising client awareness of the hazards of impulsive decision making and encouraging a more thorough evaluation of options, therapists teach clients how to improve the quality of their future decisions. Despite its many strengths, there is no guarantee that all the decisions a person makes in life using a cost–benefit analysis will prove maximally beneficial, because values and expectancies must also be taken into account when attempting to maximize the productivity of the decision-making process.

Values, according to lifestyle theory, are the general standards, ideals, and qualities perceived by the individual as desirable; rules are the customs and directives that support values; and priorities are the behavioral outcomes of rules. Through knowledge of a client's priorities, the therapist gains an appreciation of the values and rules that govern the person's behavior. The Values Inventory (see Appendix H) lists 20 general priorities that are rated on a four-point scale designed to reflect the perceived value of each priority (0 = no value, 1 = low value, 2 = moderate value, 3 = high value). The sum of the 20 ratings is postulated to represent the respondent's relative investment in four value clusters (social, work, visceral, intellectual). It is not the absolute level of each value cluster, but the relative balance between the four clusters, that is of prime concern to the lifestyle therapist. This is based on the belief that balance is the key to adaptation and that all four value clusters are required for effective decision making. Problems consequently arise when one or more of the value clusters predominates. For persons preoccupied with a drug or criminal lifestyle it is often the visceral cluster that predominates, although the goal of intervention is to balance the clusters rather than eliminate visceral values. The drug and criminal lifestyles have a tendency to distance people from their value systems by virtue of their all-consuming nature. Under such circumstances all that may be required is a realignment of behavioral priorities and values—a feat that can often be accomplished with a program of values clarification. A values clarification intervention is designed to make the client aware of discrepancies between his or her stated values and current behavioral priorities. With clients who lack certain fundamental value skills, however, more is required. Such deficits necessitate differential assessment (see Figure 6.2) and a more intensive program of intervention (see Table 6.1).

Figure 6.2 Relationships between the eight value skills and four value clusters. (Copyright Taylor & Francis, 1996; reproduced with permission.)

Goal networks comprise both goals and expectancies. Goals are the objectives a person pursues in life and expectancies are the perceived consequences and probabilities of achieving these goals. The positive and negative consequences of drug use and crime are not given equal weight by those engaged in a drug or criminal lifestyle, because the negative consequences (loss of family, incarceration) are often less immediate and frequently perceived to be less probable than the positive consequences (pleasant feelings, financial gain) (Leigh & Stacy, 1993). Expectations of enhanced social and cognitive functioning, two common short-term positive expectancies for drinking, were found to predict the alcohol consumption practices of conduct-disordered adolescents (Greenbaum, Brown, & Friedman, 1995). These expectancies may also mediate the effect of other variables (delinquency, family history) on alcohol use. In working with expectancies the objective is to consider the positive and negative, long- and short-term consequences of a behavior in a balanced appraisal of alternatives. The therapist can facilitate this process by having clients list the anticipated positive short-term, positive long-term, negative short-term, and negative long-term consequences of drug use and crime and then rate the anticipated likelihood of each consequence's occurrence on a scale from 1 to 10: 10 indicating a high likelihood that the consequence will occur and 1 a high likelihood that the consequence will not occur. The results should then be reviewed with the therapist. However, before expectancies can be modified the client's time horizon (Wilson & Herrnstein, 1985) may need to be extended. This can be accomplished by encouraging clients to identify long-range goals, trace these goals to intermediate- and short-range objectives, and then select

Table 6.1. Proposed interventions for value skill deficits

Value skill	Suggested interventions
Honesty	Advise client of the importance of honesty and how dishonesty supports a drug/criminal lifestyle; teach client the difference between fact and fiction and how to identify self-deception; reinforce client when he or she tells a verifiable truth.
Relatedness	Instruction in basic social skills; remove barriers to social interaction (e.g., anxiety, irrational thinking, lack of self-confidence); encourage involvement with others by reinforcing successive approximations to the target behavior.
Disclosure	Demonstrate the value of multichannel communication; instruction in basic listening skills; teach client how to negotiate; establish an environment in which client feels comfortable sharing his or her "secret" thoughts and ideas.
Responsibility	Teach client the value of responsibility and the role of accountability in future success; break tasks down into manageable units; show the consequences of behavior through behavioral contracts and other forms of contingency management; reinforce responsibility when it occurs.
Industriousness	Demonstrate the value of hard work for building good psychological and medical health; reframe work as an expression of one's humanity with the capacity to inject meaning into one's life; job skills training; provide opportunities for working in areas that are of interest to client.
Sentience	Educate client about the importance of understanding and using internal messages like feelings and sensations; sensitivity training; breathing exercises and other forms of deep muscle relaxation; yoga; meditation.
Concurrence	Help client appreciate the reality of change and that physical and psychological survival depends on a person's ability to adapt; teach client how to suspend judgement and attend to information supplied by the environment (including other people) rather than jumping to conclusions; learn to entertain multiple options toward a goal of increased cognitive flexibility.
Erudition	Stress and illustrate the value of knowledge in meeting the demands of everyday living; establish opportunities for new learning that are fun and rewarding; encourage and reinforce self-initiated attempts to acquire new information.

behavioral strategies capable of actualizing each goal using a cost–benefit analysis of the expected outcomes for each strategy.

COGNITION-BASED VEHICLES

Belief systems are of vital significance in understanding cognition-based vehicles of change. Borrowing from Piaget's (1963) ideas on human cognitive development, lifestyle theory defines beliefs systems as generalized schemas that help the person make sense of the surrounding environment. These schemas, which can be viewed as a person's cognitive representation of reality, are established and broadened through the interrelated action of assimilation and accommodation. Assimilation involves incorporating new information into an existing schema, whereas accommodation requires modification of a schema to account for information that has not yet been logged into a schema. Accommodation consequently involves construction, and assimilation defense. As described in Chapter 4, constructions can be classified as mythical, empirical, teleological, and epistemological and defenses as denial, distortion, diversion, and justification. Adaptation is marked by a balanced interaction of constructional and defensive functions and a balance within each function. Constructions and defenses contribute equally to adaptive living in that constructions create a belief system that defenses subsequently support, extend, and apply. People with strong allegiance to a lifestyle, however, possess belief systems—the self- and world-views being two of the more important belief systems—that are nearly exclusively rooted in mythical constructions and rigid defenses. Lifestyle thinking consequently relies on assimilation to the detriment of accommodation, whereas adaptive thinking flexibly incorporates both elements into its systems of belief. Cognitive vehicles of change are designed to promote adaptability by establishing greater balance between and within belief systems.

Cognitive Restructuring

Cognitive restructuring entails challenging a belief system and constructing a more rational or life-affirming alternative. Since there are two primary avenues by which belief systems contribute to the development of a lifestyle, there are two primary targets for cognitive restructuring. One target of a cognitive restructuring intervention is the imbalance that sometimes develops between the four categories of construction. Belief systems dominated by one category of construction—e.g., mythical constructs—are subject to what are known as constructional errors. Beck, Wright, Newman, and Liese (1993) have identified six such errors in their

work with substance-abusing clients: arbitrary inference (offering a con-
clusion without supporting evidence or in the face of contradictory evidence), dichotomous reasoning (reconceptualizing complex issues in
simplified, black-and-white terms), magnification (overemphasizing the
importance of a single event), minimization (underemphasizing the
importance of an event or behavior), overgeneralization (drawing an inference from an isolated occurrence), and personalization (inappropriately
relating external events to oneself). The steps that need to be taken in
intervening with clients who display evidence of one or more of these constructional errors is to identify and label the error, challenge the thinking behind the error, and help the client find a more rational alternative.
A procedure helpful in identifying constructional errors is to have clients
self-monitor their thinking for a period of time and chart when they entertain each one of these six constructional errors. The thoughts can then
be disputed using a formal rational challenge. The most common challenge is to ask clients to supply evidence in support of their ideas (which
is typically effective because there is little or no empirical justification
for many of these thoughts). Once a constructional error is effectively
challenged it needs to be replaced by a more rational alternative.

A second way belief systems contribute to lifestyle development is by
creating an imbalance between the defensive and constructive functions
and the four categories of each function. The end result is a series of constructional errors, a preponderance of unchecked mythical beliefs, and a
rigid pattern of defense. These three trends merge to form a series of
thinking styles—of which definitions, examples, and suggested interventions are provided in Table 6.2. The first step in intervening with these
cognitive patterns is to identify the one or two styles that are most prominent in the client's thinking. With identification of the predominant
styles, the client is in a position to challenge these patterns before they
have had an opportunity to reinforce, draw out, and fuel additional errors
and styles of thinking. One or two thinking styles are easier to challenge
than seven or eight. The Psychological Inventory of Criminal Thinking
Styles (PICTS) and Psychological Inventory of Drug-based Thinking
Styles (PIDTS) can be used to assess the eight thinking patterns. The
PICTS and PIDTS, along with the scoring criteria for both measures, are
reproduced in Appendices I, J, and K, respectively. Even though the two
instruments have similar, and in some cases identical, item content, it is
recommended that both be administered to substance-abusing criminal
offenders because different patterns of scale elevation may surface
depending on the behavior the thinking is designed to support. Once the
pertinent thinking styles have been identified, the therapist can then
establish a program of intervention. Recommended interventions for the
eight thinking styles are outlined in the final column of Table 6.2.

Table 6.2. Definitions, examples, and suggested interventions for the eight thinking styles

Thinking style	Definition	Example	Suggested intervention
Mollification	Justifying and rationalizing one's actions based on certain external considerations.	"Selling drugs is no big deal, if I didn't do it someone else would."	Focus on personal responsibility, confronting rationalizations with facts and self-deception with feedback.
Cutoff	Rapid elimination of deterrents to acting out or irresponsible behavior.	"Fuck it, I'm going to get high, I don't care what anybody says."	Develop self-control as a way of preventing the build-up of emotion that leads to cutoff; coping skills training.
Entitlement	Sense of ownership or privilege; misidentification of wants as needs.	"They locked me away for five years, now I'll get mine; they owe me."	Directly challenge attitude of ownership and privilege; teach client to discriminate between wants and needs; avoid relying on concepts like addiction that appear to fuel entitlement.
Power orientation	Exerting power and control over the external environment or one's own mood.	"I like being the center of attention and whenever I have drugs I am."	Encourage self-discipline and development of an internal locus of control; response prevention; provision of alternatives to dealing with zero state feelings.
Sentimentality	Performing various "good deeds" in an effort to portray oneself as a "good guy" despite prior wrong-doing.	"I really am a good person; even though I am a burglar I do a lot of nice things like taking the kids in the neighborhood out for ice cream."	Ask the client to list the positive and negative consequences of lifestyle and ask if positive consequences logically erase the negative ones; teach the client how to discriminate between sentimentality and true caring and concern.

Continued

Table 6.2. (*Continued*)

Thinking style	Definition	Example	Suggested intervention
Superoptimism	An unrealistic belief in being able to indefinitely escape the negative consequences of a drug or criminal lifestyle.	"I can stop drinking whenever I want, I'm just not ready to stop."	Confront the unrealistic expectations and beliefs that underpin superoptimism; to demonstrate the fallacy of superoptimism, use the fact that some clients with similar beliefs are currently incarcerated or in trouble with the law.
Cognitive indolence	Lazy, uncritical thinking in which the subject takes a great many "short-cuts."	"Why work or go to school when its easier to just steal."	Critical reasoning skills training; goal-setting, particularly as this relates to establishing and linking short-, intermediate-, and long-range goals.
Discontinuity	Lack of consistency or congruence in one's thinking and behavior.	"I normally start out with the best of intentions but have been known to lose track of these intentions over time."	Continual feedback and self-monitoring of all thoughts within a specified time period (e.g., 10 minutes every evening); identify compartmentalization (Jekyll and Hyde Syndrome) and provide client with a structured intervention in which concrete issues and topics are introduced by the therapist.

Note: The reader should consult Walters (1990, 1994b, 1996c) and Yochelson and Samenow (1976) for more information on these thinking styles.

Cognitive Reframing

Some people take an optimistic view of the world, while others tend to be more pessimistic. This has a great deal to do with the thoughts people have toward themselves and others. Cognitive reframing entails encouraging clients to adopt a perspective different from the one they currently profess. Marlatt and Gordon (1985) claim that a slip attributed to external, unstable, specific, and controllable factors is much less likely to lead to relapse than a slip attributed to internal, stable, global, and uncontrollable factors. With the possible exception of the internal–external attribution, research tends to support this view (Collins & Lapp, 1991; Grilo & Shiffman, 1994). Changing the attributions for a lapse from signs of imminent failure to opportunities for new learning can consequently reduce the probability of future relapse. Cognitive reframing, whether the target is a lapse or other event, begins with an examination of the negative aspects of the client's situation or concern. This is followed by identification of the proverbial "silver lining" in which the client reflects on the positive features of a situation or concern. Owing to the negative mindset of many clients the therapist may need to guide clients through the process, encouraging them to focus on as many positive aspects as possible. Once the "silver lining" has been identified, clients should be asked which interpretation, positive or negative, is most likely to put them in a position to achieve their long- and short-terms goals, avoid conflict with others, and feel the way they want to feel (Maultsby, 1975). The emphasis needs to be on the fact that while there is no single "correct" way to interpret a stimulus, event, or behavior, adopting an attitude which facilitates future success makes more sense than accepting one that leads to anger, depression, and failure.

CHAPTER 7

Finding a Reinforcing Non-drug/Non-criminal Lifestyle

The drug and criminal lifestyles can be traced back to both successful and unsuccessful socialization. As the reader may recall, socialization is the process by which a person internalizes the rules, norms, and values of a society, culture, or group. Failure to socialize to conventional definitions of behavior plays a key role in the embryonic development of a drug or criminal lifestyle (Hirschi, 1969). However, these lifestyles would not exist if it were not for an equally powerful socialization to deviant definitions of behavior acquired through association with those already involved in the lifestyle (Sutherland & Cressey, 1978). Weak socialization to conventional definitions of behavior and strong socialization to deviant definitions of behavior coalesce to create the conditions that give birth to a drug or criminal lifestyle. Resocialization to new definitions of behavior is therefore required to counteract these effects and solidify gains made during the first two phases of intervention. Like socialization, resocialization is based on patterns of involvement, commitment, and identification. However, whereas socialization to a drug or criminal lifestyle signifies a growing preoccupation, commitment, and identification with drugs and crime, resocialization symbolizes involvement in lifestyle-incongruent activities and relationships, commitment to goals incompatible with a drug or criminal lifestyle, and identification with something other than drugs and crime. Resocialization is more than an adjustment in lifestyle (e.g., using a note instead of a gun when robbing a bank) or a swapping of lifestyles (e.g., switching from a drug lifestyle to a Narcotics Anonymous lifestyle). Resocialization requires that the individual change his or her actions, goals, and identity.

The primary objective of resocialization is to expand a client's adaptive resources. Although consummate adaptability is unrealistic (given the fact that all people engage in some lifestyle behavior), people can nevertheless broaden their repertoire of adaptive skills. As was noted in Chapter 2, there are three general categories of response to existential fear; the most primitive being despair. Despair is often expressed as terror or confusion and frequently leads to anxiety and depression and, in extreme cases, suicide and psychosis. A second general category of response to existential fear is a repeated pattern of behavior designed to foster relief, reassurance, and a sense of personal control. This is commonly referred to as the lifestyle response. A third way people respond to existential fear is by altering their thoughts, feelings, and actions in an effort to comprehend rather than manipulate their environment. Lifestyle theory considers this particular response a sign of adaptation. Over the course of a day most people display all three categories of response, the sum total of a person's daily experience being classified as his or her lifestyle. The goal of lifestyle intervention is to encourage reduced reliance on patterned activities and increased involvement in adaptive pursuits. As Figure 7.1 illustrates, higher functioning lifestyles are characterized by greater adaptability and less reliance on patterned behavior than lower functioning lifestyles. One additional benefit of expanding one's adaptive resources is reduced despair, for as people begin to comprehend the surrounding environment there is less opportunity or incentive for despair.

Self-organization is a principle derived from chaos theory to describe the process by which complicated patterns and structures emerge from open systems following a period of instability or turbulence (Barton, 1994). These patterns and structures appear to occur without direct input

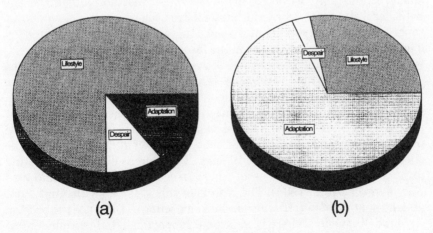

(a)   (b)

Figure 7.1. Comparison of (a) lower and (b) higher functioning lifestyles

from the external environment. Based on the observation that most people abandon a drug or criminal lifestyle without external (professional) assistance (McMurran, 1994; Walters, 1998), it could be argued that self-organization is a powerful force behind the resocialization process. The lifestyle model assumes that all change is self-change and that the therapist's primary function is to nurture the client's capacity for self-organization—a capacity the client shares with all human beings. In partial support of this claim, medical researchers have shown that instability, flexibility, and self-organization are vital to human survival. While a moderately unstable heart rate and EEG portend good physical health, a steady heart rate or predictable EEG often precedes the onset of a heart attack or epileptic seizure, respectively (Gleick, 1987). A system must possess the capacity to respond across a wide range of situations and conditions or risk extinction. According to proponents of chaos theory, any system that remains locked on a single frequency, channel, or pattern will have trouble responding effectively to environmental challenge. An organism's survival depends on its ability to generate multiple forms and organize these forms into a congruent and meaningful whole. The role of self-organization in resocialization is described further in discussions on involvement, commitment, and identification, the three component features of socialization and resocialization.

INVOLVEMENT

Lifestyles are construed as caricatures, prototypes, and ideals that people approach rather than concrete entities that people achieve. Lifestyles should consequently be viewed in relative rather than absolute terms. The behavioral styles described in Chapter 4 are used to assess a person's distance from the lifestyle caricature since these styles are believed to reflect a person's level of involvement in the lifestyle. Involvement encompasses two general sets of behaviors: the activities a person engages in and the social relationships he or she entertains. As a lifestyle progresses there is a tendency for initial involvement to transform into a growing preoccupation with lifestyle-related activities and relationships. Involvement also sheds light on the drug–crime overlap. Findings from a study of 506 urban adolescent males indicate that involvement in property crime encourages involvement in illegal drug use, whereas illegal drug use and drug dealing elevate the risk of committing person-related crime (van Kamman & Loeber, 1994). The results of this study also insinuate that discontinuation of illegal drug use or drug dealing may reduce the propensity for delinquency. There is additional support for a bidirectional interpretation of drug–crime involvement in a study by Anglin, Brecht,

Woodward, and Bonett (1986). In this study continued involvement in drug-related criminal activity suppressed the natural maturing out of drug use process ordinarily observed in drug users over time. Interventions for substance-abusing criminal offenders must accordingly address both drug and criminal involvements since each appears capable of stimulating the other.

Resocialization entails shifting one's involvements from drugs and crime to activities and relationships incompatible with the drug and criminal lifestyles. This process necessitates a change in lifestyle, whereby the person abandons drug- and crime-related activities and associations in favor of non-drug/non-criminal activities and associations. From the results of interviews conducted with persons self-remitting from alcohol, tobacco, and opiates, Stall and Biernacki (1986) concluded that substitute activities such as jogging, meditation, and work helped expedite the transition from drug use to abstinence. Along these same lines, Zimmerman and Maton (1992) discerned that compensatory activities such as school attendance and church involvement exerted a mitigating effect on drug use in African-American youth at risk for delinquent behavior and substance misuse. As these and other studies suggest, lifestyles are one way people structure their time. With the loss of a lifestyle one must find a replacement or risk returning to the lifestyle out of boredom, habit, or fear. It is for this reason that substitution is awarded a prominent position in the lifestyle model. Ideally, the substitute should be more adaptable than the lifestyle it is designed to replace. By affording clients an opportunity to develop and expand their adaptive resources the therapist lays the framework for a more adaptive alternative to a client's earlier preoccupation with drugs and crime. The degree to which adaptive behaviors and pursuits replace old lifestyle patterns and rituals is one estimate of the success of resocialization since adaptability helps people transcend their current situations and achieve personal growth through self-organization.

The substitution process follows a simple three-step procedure. The first step is to identify the wants, wishes, and desires being met by a drug or criminal lifestyle. This can be accomplished by having clients list the activities, associations, and feelings they believe they will miss should they decide to abandon a drug or criminal lifestyle. Once the list has been constructed the next step is to assist clients in selecting substitute activities designed to satisfy the wants, wishes, and desires previously fulfilled by the old lifestyle. Effort needs to be directed at developing hobbies, interests, relationships, and activities that contribute to a more adaptable lifestyle. The third step in the change process is to encourage clients to put these alternative behaviors into action. By virtue of their prior exposure to the attribution triad, clients understand that change is difficult and somewhat alien to them. It has been estimated that it takes several months of repeated performance of an unfamiliar behavior before that behavior begins, to feel "comfortable" to the individual (Marlatt & George, 1984). This is why the lifestyle model advocates behavioral contracting with the stipulation that therapists regularly review the contract with clients. This is done in order to assure compliance with the conditions of the contract and determine whether the contract requires modification. It may be possible to stimulate involvement and commitment (the second component of the resocialization process) to a new lifestyle by having the client identify and work on accomplishing a daily task that ties into his or her eventual goal of finding a non-drug/non-criminal lifestyle.

COMMITMENT

Commitment is the second component of the socialization/resocialization process. This particular component of resocialization is concerned with identifying and validating the goals that people pursue in formulating a new lifestyle. Creating a commitment to change is the principal aim of the foundational phase of intervention in which arresting the lifestyle assumes center stage. Commitment to a new way of life, on the other hand, becomes progressively more important as intervention proceeds. People who commit to a drug or criminal lifestyle are often attracted to the short-term pleasure that drugs and crime provide. Committing to something other than a drug or criminal lifestyle accordingly requires a shift in goals, expectancies, values, and priorities. The individual must select new goals based on a thorough evaluation of the perceived consequences of his or her actions and then construct a value system incompatible with his or her continued involvement with drugs and crime. Investigating the process by which people commit to self-help groups like Alcoholics Anonymous, Donovan (1984) found support for Rosabeth Moss Kanter's (1972) conceptual framework of commitment generation. Kanter describes six processes in her theory of how commitment to voluntary organizations like Alcoholics Anonymous and Rational Recovery is generated and maintained: sacrifice, renunciation, investment, communion, mortification, and transcendence (see Figure 7.2). The remaining paragraphs of this section are devoted to a review of how these processes can facilitate commitment to a new lifestyle.

Sacrifice, the first of the Kanterian processes described by Donovan (1984), necessitates abandoning the pleasures provided by a valued object or outcome in exchange for the opportunity to achieve a greater end. Before one can commit to a new lifestyle one must be willing to forfeit the short-term pleasure and hedonism of a drug or criminal lifestyle. This

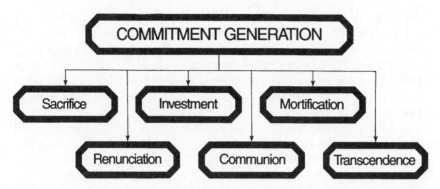

Figure 7.2. The six processes cited in Rosabeth Moss Kanter's commitment generation model

can be accomplished, in part, by conducting a cost–benefit analysis in which the costs (delayed gratification) and benefits (long-term satisfaction) of a non-drug or non-criminal lifestyle are contrasted with the costs (long-term harm) and benefits (immediate gratification) of a drug or criminal lifestyle. Commitment commences with a willingness to relinquish the benefits that might reasonably be anticipated from involvement in drug and criminal activity. Positive rituals, one of the factors that encourage development of a shaman effect, can help soothe the discomfort of sacrifice and confer meaning to the sacrificial act. Whether the ritual involves tossing one's last pack of cigarettes into the garbage can or throwing one's scrapbook of criminal memorabilia into the fire, it personifies the loss–purification–reformation cycle that ultimately encourages resocialization through self-organization. The therapist can facilitate this process by highlighting the value and necessity of sacrifice, exploring the specific benefits that can reasonably be anticipated from sacrifice, and leading clients through a series of purification and empowerment rituals designed to stimulate a preliminary commitment to a new lifestyle. Sacrifice and positive ritual, it would seem, are necessary prerequisites for commitment to a new way of life.

Renunciation symbolizes one's willingness to forsake drug- and crime-related interpersonal relationships (Kanter, 1972). Avoidance of former drug and criminal associates, however, must be accompanied by a growing awareness of the self-defeating nature of these relationships. Besides renouncing old alliances, the client must also explore, establish, and invest in new friendships, for this too contributes to commitment. Research indicates that a lack of conventional social support portends poor outcomes in persons who abuse substances (Booth, Russell, Soucek, & Laughlin, 1992) and engage in habitual delinquency (Hammersley, Forsyth, &

Lavelle, 1990). Two successful models of intervention—the community reinforcement approach (Higgins, Budney, Bickel, & Badger, 1994) and multisystemic therapy (Henggeler, Borduin, Melton, Mann, Smith, Hall, Cone, & Fucci, 1991)—both incorporate social support and skill building into their procedures. If the client has no visible means of social support then a support system must be found. Twelve-step programs provide opportunities for support through use of a sponsor system. The fourth process cited by Kanter (1972) in her explication of the commitment process to voluntary organizations is the community that flows from social support. This process, termed communion by Kanter, fills the void created by renunciation and abandonment of a drug or criminal lifestyle.

The final two mechanisms described by Kanter (1972), mortification and transcendence, touch on the issue of identity and blend well with the identification component of the overall resocialization process. Mortification is defined as losing oneself in the supporting group, whereas transcendence entails finding oneself through a growing identification with the supporting group (Kanter, 1972). Lifestyle theorists consider self-identity to be as important as group-identity and endorse efforts to find meaning in the merging of these two forces, which, incidentally, are viewed as two sides of the same coin. Logotherapy (Frankl, 1984) is a method of intervention that emphasizes meaning and purpose in life. A recent study, in fact, suggests that purpose in life may predict future drug and alcohol involvement in persons released from substance-abuse programming. Relapse was substantially lower in a three-month follow-up of high purpose-in-life subjects graduating from a skill-based substance-abuse program but was accelerated in high purpose-in-life subjects completing an authoritarian, confrontational program (Waisberg & Porter, 1994). These findings connote that meaning in life may predict positive outcomes only so far as there is something tangible on which to base one's new-found purpose in life (i.e., skills). Helping clients find meaning in life can therefore be of major consequence in strengthening commitment to a new lifestyle, provided this is accompanied by a growing introspective attitude, new skill development, and changes in both the client's involvements and identification.

IDENTIFICATION

Identification is the third major component of the socialization and reso-cialization processes. As a person's involvement with drugs and crime grows so, too, does his or her identification with drug and criminal behavior. Labeling oneself an alcoholic, addict, hustler, drug dealer, or bank robber encourages expanded involvement in and commitment to these lifestyles by way of increased identification with the behavior. However, identity is an exceedingly complex and elusive phenomenon that impacts on a person's behavior in disparate ways. Walters (1996a), for instance, reports that identity can either facilitate or inhibit addictive involvement. Identity may facilitate drug and criminal involvement by providing an identity for those in search of a self-image, limiting a person's access to alternative behaviors and relationships, and encouraging a mindset that improves one's chances of relapse. Identity can also inhibit involvement in drug and criminal behavior. Studies show, for instance, that clients who avoid self-labeling are in a better position to moderate and control their drinking than clients who identify themselves as alcoholics or problem drinkers (Miller, Leckman, Delaney, & Tinkcom, 1992). In a second study, personal crises stimulated a preliminary desire for change in persons previously dependent on heroin, but a transformation in identity was seen as instrumental in maintaining that change (Andersson, Nilsson, & Tunving, 1983). Finally, identity transformation often accompanies unassisted change in persons previously involved with alcohol (Tuchfeld, 1981), heroin (Klingemann, 1991), and crime (Cusson & Pinsonneault, 1986). Resocialization must therefore be accompanied by a change in identity.

The identity transformation process that supports socialization to a drug or criminal lifestyle can be insidious. Even though it may be necessary to sentence some substance-abusing offenders to jail or prison, this can become an additional source of deviant socialization that interferes with the person's ability to resocialize to an alternative way of life. Prisonization is one influence that can encourage increased socialization to a drug or criminal lifestyle by virtue of its impact on identity. The prisonization concept is defined as a person's acceptance of the rules, norms, and values of the wider prison culture (Thomas & Peterson, 1977). The effects of prisonization can be so pernicious that some programs, particularly those that follow the therapeutic community (TC) approach, attempt to separate their clients from the general inmate population. Utilizing four different measures of prisonization—inmate code adoption, custody staff rejection, caseworker rejection, mental health staff rejection—Peat and Winfree (1992) were able to demonstrate that TC participants achieved significantly lower prisonization scores than general-population inmates and a group of waiting-list controls. In addition, the amount of time subjects spent in the TC was inversely proportional to their scores on these four measures of prisonization. Additional research is required before the clinical significance of these findings can be determined, but one possibility is that involvement in a TC promotes identity changes that shield the individual from the nefarious effects of prisonization.

The initial step in interventions targeting identity is to secure an accurate estimate of the client's self-view. This can be achieved with the aid of the Bipolar Identity Survey (see Appendix L). Lifestyle theory assumes that constructions derive from the dialectic transformation of bipolar concepts (e.g., me–not me; good–not good). Although the schemas and self-schemas that emanate out of a person's efforts to comprehend the world grow in complexity and integration over time, it is possible to assess the content of specific schemas and the overall structure of the self-system using the Bipolar Identity Survey. This survey can be helpful in gauging the content of specific self-schema and in evaluating the structure of the entire self-system. The content of self-schema is difficult to categorize because it is so unique and individualized. The structure of the self-system, on the other hand, is more amenable to evaluation since it is believed to vary along three primary dimensions. The first dimension of the self-system structure concerns the degree to which self-schema are positive or negative. Positive self-schema offer a favorable evaluation of skills, abilities, and attributes, while negative self-schema render a less favorable evaluation of these same skills, abilities, and attributes. The second dimension focuses on the complexity of individual schema. Whereas simple schema tend to be global and undifferentiated, complex schema are more individualized, situationally specific, and intricate. System organization is the third dimension along which self-systems vary. A fragmented self-system comprises unconnected categories or compartments of experience, whereas the self-schema in an integrated self-system are meaningfully linked and generally well organized. These three dimensions are illustrated in Figure 7.3.

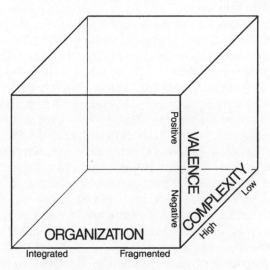

Figure 7.3. The three dimensions of the self-system structure

Identity transformation is one of the main objectives of resocialization. Experience dictates that transformation rests on a client's willingness to entertain and embrace a set of behaviors, values, and expectancies different from those that define his or her prior preoccupation with drugs or crime. This, along with the successes a person records once newly acquired skills are implemented, can positively affect the valence dimension of the self-system. Lifestyle therapists also encourage clients to enlarge the complexity of their self-schema since studies show that cognitive complexity can inoculate people against the debilitating effects of stress (Linville, 1987), depression (Dance & Kuiper, 1987), and frustration (Dixon & Baumeister, 1991). Cognitive complexity can be solicited by engaging clients in Socratic dialogue (Frankl, 1984) or by reinforcing their cognitive restructuring skills (Ellis, 1970). The goal of interventions directed at the identity component of resocialization is to augment the complexity and situational specificity of a client's self-schema (perhaps by encouraging the client to base his or her identity on specific behaviors rather than global characteristics) given that simple and global schemata supply people with many fewer options than complex and situationally specific schemata. Situationally specific self-schema are believed to be more adaptable than global self-schema and an integrated self-system is said to be more adaptable than a fragmented one. Another major goal of intervention, then, is to enhance the integration of the overall self-system—no small task in someone with a fragmented and highly compartmentalized self-view. However, by encouraging greater self-observation, perhaps with the aid of videotaped replays of group interactions (Skafte, 1987), the therapist can afford clients an opportunity to erect a more balanced, integrated, and organized self-system.

Introducing information incompatible with a client's current self-view can create cognitive dissonance that might then be used to encourage development of more cognitively complex and situationally specific self-schema. The dialectic method can also be used to expand the self-system through its ability to increase cognitive complexity and promote schematic integration. As was mentioned in Chapter 5, the dialectic method involves taking an idea (thesis), contrasting it with its polar opposite (antithesis), and then synthesizing the two ideas into a meaningful whole. Whether the emphasis is on involvement, commitment, or identification, all three components of resocialization tie into self-organization in some way. By avoiding growth-inhibiting labels and challenging tired old ideas the therapist can generate momentary system instability. This is often the approach utilized by structural family therapists. Since open systems have been known to self-organize after a period of disequilibrium, new schema and self-schema will eventually form. Whether these new schema are more positive, complex, and integrated than those they replace will depend, to a large extent, on the materials used in their construction. If involvement, commitment, and identity materials are guided by a basic respect for oneself, others, and the surrounding environment (the so-called universal laws of adaptability) and supported by a mature sense of self-confidence and new skill development, then self-organization will likely to result in a more adaptable outcome. Conversely, if these materials are based on disrespect, arrogance, or fantasy, then self-organization will lead a new outcome that may be no more adaptable than that which it is designed to replace.

CHAPTER 8

Putting It All Together

The three phases of lifestyle intervention are suggestive rather than injunctive. It is therefore imperative that therapists refrain from falling into the trap of scripting. Scripting denotes rigid enactment of a specific sequence of interventions or the creation of a universal format for therapy. According to lifestyle theory, there is no such thing as a blueprint for change. Therapists can assist in the change process by helping clients forge their own exodus from a drug or criminal lifestyle. Reminiscent of how Prochaska and DiClemente (1992) envisioned their stages of change, the phases of lifestyle intervention are construed as guides to relevant issues, concerns, and goals for intervention. This, of course, requires an adequate repertoire of strategies and the wisdom to know how, when, and where to apply these strategies. A therapist's repertoire of interventions may include methods outlined in Chapters 5, 6, and 7 of this text, methods the therapist has found effective in his or her own clinical work with clients, or both. However, to avoid the fragmentation that occurs with the use of highly specialized techniques (e.g., rational restructuring for thinking errors, role playing for assertiveness), therapists might also want to consider employing general strategies of intervention to supplement the specific strategies that often serve as the first line of intervention with clients.

GENERAL STRATEGIES OF INTERVENTION

Whereas specific strategies of intervention tie into specific change vehicles, general strategies address several different vehicles at the same time. Four such strategies are described in this section: therapist attitude, spirituality, visualization, and mentoring.

Therapist Attitude

The goal of early phase intervention is to arrest the lifestyle and extend the arresting process. As defined in Chapter 5, the shaman effect is one way this can be achieved. The shaman effect, as the reader may recall, is an outgrowth of the client–therapist relationship assisted by certain therapist actions. The attitude believed to be most conducive to the creation of a shaman effect is said to reflect sensitivity, positive ritual, metaphor, dialectics, and the attribution triad. There are many ways to demonstrate sensitivity, from expertise to interpretation, one of the more common being to uphold the Rogerian ideals of genuineness, empathy, and unconditional positive regard (Rogers, 1957). The reliability, consistency, and structure of therapy sessions likewise supply fertile soil for development of the positive rituals. The informed and reasoned use of metaphor and dialectics also contribute to the formation of a shaman effect, as does the responsibility, hope, and empowerment engendered by the attribution triad.

Spirituality

The power of belief and myth should not be overlooked in our haste to apply individual techniques. A sense of connectiveness to something greater than ourselves can provide people with the opportunity to transcend their individual life circumstances and problems. Nature, religion, and community are three primary sources of connectiveness or collectivity. Collectivity implies an extension of the life instinct to other people (community), to the non-human environment (nature), and to certain values, principles, and ideals (religion). Twelve-step programs emphasize spirituality but are only one of the ways clients can achieve a sense of collectivity. Spiritual goals can also be realized through social support and a person's genuine desire to commune with nature. Spirituality not only encourages transcendence but also provides opportunities for development of life meaning by molding disparate interventions into an organized whole through the integrative action of a core theme or ideal.

Visualization

Visualization is a third general strategy with clear integrative capabilities. Patrick Fanning (1994) has written a book on visualization in which he describes the use of visualization techniques. Visualization is a skill worth learning and Fanning's book does a nice job illustrating how effective visualization can be accomplished. However, visualization is also addressed in media presentations of drug abuse and crime. Motion pictures provide a particularly valuable visualization technique, because movies of a drug or criminal nature frequently embody the caricature of a drug or criminal lifestyle unencumbered by the constraints imposed by a reality that makes it impossible for any one person to discharge the roles of the lifestyle 24 hours a day. Additionally, motion pictures cover issues pertinent to all three phases of lifestyle intervention (foundation, vehicles, non-drug/non-criminal lifestyle). Whether the focus is on the drug lifestyle ("Clean and Sober"), criminal lifestyle ("Straight Time"), or both ("Drug Store Cowboy"), such interventions are capable of integrating images and ideas through the coordinating action of universal themes. Besides encouraging clients to identify the thinking patterns as they occur in a movie, the therapist can pose questions to clients (see Table 8.1) in an effort to get at crucial lifestyle issues.

Mentoring

Lifestyle intervention is often conducted in groups. The reasoning behind this general practice is twofold. First, it provides novice clients with the

Table 8.1. Questions pertaining to three drug- and crime-related movies

Clean and Sober (1988)—starring Michael Keaton (124 minutes)

Q1. What were Daryl Poynter's initial motives for entering rehab and did these motives change over the course of the movie?
Q2. This movie portrays several myths that have worked their way into the twelve-step philosophy. What are they?
Q3. What problems confronted Daryl upon his release from rehab?
Q4. What role did social support play in Daryl's life after rehab?
Q5. What does Lenny represent to Charlie? (*Note:* Lenny can serve as a metaphor for factors that potentially lead back to a drug lifestyle.) What is your own personal Lenny?

Drugstore Cowboy (1989)—starring Matt Dillon (104 minutes)

Q1. What does Bob Hughes' "crew" symbolize for him?
Q2. Identify examples of interpersonal triviality portrayed in this movie.
Q3. Explain what the "open transom" scene reveals about opportunity.
Q4. What do you believe will happen once Bob arrives at the hospital at the end of the movie?
Q5. What does Bob Hughes mean by "all you gotta do is look at the labels on the little bottles" in describing what he sees as the benefits of a drug lifestyle.

Straight Time (1978)—starring Dustin Hoffman (114 minutes)

Q1. What role did the parole officer play in Max Dembo's eventual decision to return to crime?
Q2. What role did Max Dembo play in his own demise? What choices did he make?
Q3. Identify the social skills that Max appears to lack and offer possible remedies.
Q4. How honest was Max with his girlfriend? How honest was he with himself?
Q5. Was Max justified in killing Willie, the driver of the getaway car? What are the likely consequences of his actions?

opportunity to learn from peers who are further along in the change process than they. Second, discussing common issues and concerns in a group setting can often help clients overcome feelings of isolation, alienation, and abnormality. It is suggested that these groups be as heterogeneous as possible, because groups replete with precontemplative clients frequently degenerate into power struggles between the therapist and participants who want to convince the therapist that change is infeasible, unrealistic, or unattainable. Groups dominated by maintenance stage clients, on the other hand, may assume the appearance of a revival meeting. Heterogeneous groups allow for a clear exchange of ideas and increased opportunities for learning. They also establish the proper conditions for mentoring. Mentoring is the process by which clients functioning at a later stage in the change process assist and tutor clients functioning at an earlier stage. Both parties to this relationship benefit, the early stage individual from the later stage individual's experience and the later stage individual from teaching and sharing his or her ideas with others.

CASE STUDY: WALTER

Background

Walter is a 44-year-old, married, African-American male serving a 70-month sentence for unarmed bank robbery. He states that his father, a merchant marine, died when he was young and that after his father's death his mother hosted marathon poker games to make ends meet. The gamblers, drug dealers, and street hustlers who attended these poker games fascinated him and it was not long before he was running the streets in search of their approval and acceptance. It should be noted, however, that even before being exposed to these negative role models Walter found the outlaw mentality appealing (e.g., identifying with and rooting for the "bad guys" in the movies). Another important early life event that may have helped shape his self- and world-views was a hip injury suffered in early adolescence. He was prescribed morphine for the pain but believes that he was not properly detoxified following his release from the hospital. Walter enjoyed the pleasurable sensations that morphine provided, so much so that he strove to recapture these feelings by consuming street heroin. He began snorting heroin at age 14 but was injecting it daily by the time he was 18 years of age. Although he has used a variety of different substances over the course of his life—from marijuana to cough syrup to cocaine—heroin was the drug he preferred most. Several treatment programs and multiple trials of methadone failed to curb his appetite for heroin, which he began to mix with cocaine during his mid-twenties in a concoction commonly referred to as a "speed ball." In fact, Walter indicates that he often ingested cocaine when he was on methadone because the mixture produced a continual "speed ball" effect.

Walter's first arrest occurred at age 19 when he was picked up for possession of heroin. Although subsequently arrested for assault, theft, and robbery, he avoided incarceration until age 29, when he initially served five years of a 15-year state sentence for armed robbery and passing bad checks. Upon his release from custody, Walter, who had continued using drugs in prison, began robbing banks with notes in order to support his growing heroin habit. He was soon caught and remanded to the custody of the US Attorney General where he served 5 years of an 8-year sentence in a federal penitentiary. Shortly after his release from federal custody he got married. He had earned an AA degree in prison and was working temporarily at the post office. He made several attempts to control his use of heroin and refrained from ingesting it on the job. However, over time his drug use consumed his actions and identity and overrode all personal, family, and occupational responsibilities. It did not take him long to start robbing banks again and within a year he was back in federal custody. He states that in the past he never intended to avoid drugs upon his release from incarceration and that it was not until the present incarceration that he even terminated his drug use while in prison. Three factors have contributed to his desire for change. First, he was getting older and could no longer rebound from incarceration like he had when he was younger. Second, he stated that he wants to serve as a positive role model for his daughter, age 14, and other neighborhood children. Finally, he observed a fellow heroin user from the old neighborhood who had made significant changes in his life as a consequence of his own participation in the Lifestyle Change program. All three factors were instrumental in establishing the proper motivational set for change.

Assessment

Assessment is normally accomplished within the context of a particular intervention. In order to understand the relationship between drugs and crime, however, it can be helpful to examine the DLSI and LCSF—two instruments that assess lifestyle involvement, commitment, and identification, independent of any specific interventions. Walter's DLSI results denote strong identification with the drug lifestyle (total DLSI score = 16) as characterized by high scores on the interpersonal triviality (5) and stress-coping imbalance (4) subscales, and moderately high scores on the social rule-breaking/bending (3.5) and irresponsibility/pseudoresponsibility (3) subscales. A review of Walter's pre-sentence investigation report revealed a score of 9 on the LCSF, which is just below the cutoff normally associated with lifestyle patterns of criminal conduct. These findings indicate that Walter displays significant involvement in, commitment to, and identification with the drug and criminal lifestyles, although the drug lifestyle may be more ingrained than the criminal lifestyle. The criminal lifestyle should not be ignored, however, since criminal behavior that has evolved in support of a drug lifestyle can develop independently of its drug lifestyle origins. This, in fact, is suggested in a comparison of Walter's PICTS and PIDTS results in which mollification appears to support the criminal lifestyle but the cutoff, sentimentality, superoptimism, and discontinuity protect the drug lifestyle (see Figure 8.1). Subscale analysis of the DLSI indicates that the rituals and superfluous communications that mark a drug lifestyle and the desire to eliminate stress may be maintaining Walter's lifestyle. Accordingly, resistance skills training and stress management training were awarded central positions in Walter's change plan.

Intervention

Since lifestyle theory eschews the notion of treatment, the lifestyle therapist follows a change plan rather than a treatment plan. The change plan highlights the work a client must do in order to change his or her

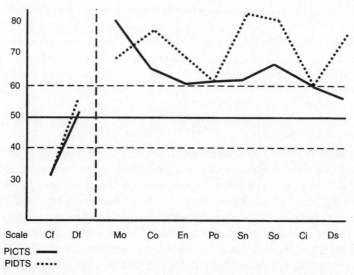

Figure 8.1. A comparison of Walter's PICTS and PIDTS results. (Abbreviations: *see* Figure 4.1.).

behavior. This can be accomplished in partnership with, or independent of, a professional therapist. Whereas treatment plans are frequently imposed on clients, change plans are developed in collaboration with clients. As such, a change plan lists options rather than mandates and considers a person's strengths as well as his or her limitations. Walter's change plan was derived from assessments and discussions showing that he had difficulty managing stress, avoiding drug-related cues and availability, and confronting the "convict code" that he has grown to accept. Among the personal strengths included in Walter's change plan were his ability to assert himself, his lateral thinking ability, and his motivation for change. Each strength was incorporated into the intervention. Walter's assertiveness helped guide development of his critical reasoning skills in that he was encouraged to apply his interpersonal assertiveness skills to his own thinking. Walter's lateral thinking ability was used to provide him with multiple options for dealing with drug-related cues, the availability of drugs, and his unquestioning acceptance of the "convict code." His motivation for change also worked its way into his change plan and was reinforced with creation of a shaman effect that relied on therapist prediction and interpretation, positive ritual, and attention to the attribution triad. This motivation, in turn, helped him move into the later phases (vehicle, non-drug/non-criminal life-style) of the change process.

The Lifestyle Stress Test revealed that a majority of Walter's stress could be attributed to intrapersonal sources of stress. As such, the therapist provided him with instruction in basic relaxation techniques, time management, and exercise as ways of reducing tension and managing stress. Values also figure prominently in Walter's change plan. With the aid of the Values Inventory Walter learned that at the height of his involvement with drugs and crime his social, work, and intellectual values were significantly weaker than his visceral values. Accordingly, values clarification and interventions designed to buttress honesty, responsibility, disclosure, and erudition were made part of his change plan. Further assessment revealed that he had previously suffered from a lack of balance between short- and long-term goals and expectancies. This was due in large part to the fact that he often emphasized the short-term positive outcomes of drug use and crime over the long-term negative consequences while on the streets. An extensive program of goal networking was instituted with Walter so that he could better balance long-, short-, and intermediate-range goals and expectancies. Within the context of the third phase of intervention he was encouraged to develop a reinforcing non-drug/non-criminal lifestyle that would help prevent him from reverting back to old destructive habits. He decided to access this new lifestyle by developing his work and occupational skills and finding a job to support himself and his family. His short-term goal may have been to find a job, but his long-term goal was to implement the Lifestyle Change program with juveniles in his community. Since participating in the Lifestyle Change program Walter has made a good adjustment, the ultimate test coming later this year when he is scheduled for release.

CASE STUDY: MARK

Background

Mark is a 19-year-old, single, white male serving an 85-month sentence for armed bank robbery. Mark's role in the instant offense consisted of holding a rifle (later determined to be a BB gun) on the patrons of the bank while his two accomplices ransacked the teller drawers. As they were leaving the bank one of the patrons attempted to intervene and Mark struck him with the butt of the rifle. Mark was arrested a week later in response to a tip from a drug dealer from whom he and his accomplices had purchased marijuana with the bank robbery money. Even though this is Mark's first adult incarceration he has been in and out of juvenile detention facilities and halfway houses since age 13. A primary motive for his involvement in the instant offense as well as other crimes he has committed is the rush of adrenalin he experiences when he takes risks: "I'm the kind of person who likes living on the edge." His first arrest occurred at age 15 when he and a friend were caught breaking into parking meters. He has also been arrested for theft, assault, and burglary, but acknowledges participation in a relatively large number of offenses for which he never got caught, including several business robberies contemporaneous to the instant offense. Mark started smoking marijuana at age 14 and states that he has tried "just about every drug except heroin." Although he acknowledges experimentation with a wide variety of substances, he prefers marijuana and such hallucinogenic agents as LSD and psilocybin (mushrooms). Never one for studying, Mark dropped out of high school prior to entering the eleventh grade. However, he earned his GED a few years later and enrolled in several college courses. Unfortunately, he was unable to complete the college classes because he ran away from the halfway house where he was residing at the time. Mark states that he has held legitimate jobs but none for more than a few months at a time.

Mark never knew his natural mother, who was in prison when he was born, or his father, who has been in and out of mental institutions. Shifted from one foster home to another, he was eventually adopted at age 6. Mark characterized his relationship with his adoptive father as strained but indicates that he got along well with his adoptive mother and two adoptive sisters. He accused his adoptive father of both physical and sexual abuse and advised that he ran away from home at age 13 after his adoptive mother became aware of the abuse. Thereafter he lived on the streets or in various shelters, group homes, and juvenile detention facilities. He described himself as a rebellious kid who enjoyed fighting. Violence is apparently how Mark deals with his angry feelings and frustrations. This has led to a series of mental hospital admissions and several suicide attempts, but he is not viewed to be the victim of mental illness; rather, he is seen as a sensitive, albeit angry, young man who has learned to manage his feelings with violence. In fact, Mark was recently transferred from another federal facility after he got into a fight with another inmate whom he beat so severely that the inmate had to be transferred to an outside hospital. Mark relates that everyone he has ever gotten close to has either died or moved away. Consequently, even though he has trouble trusting others, he exhibits a strong need for affiliation with others. He acknowledges that this has led him to become somewhat of a care-taker, fighting other people's battles and engaging in crime in order to financially support friends. Mark seems to have a particularly strong desire to be mothered and relates that while he has never been married, his girlfriend is 20 years his senior. These issues are addressed in his change plan.

Assessment

The LCSF and DLSI suggest that Mark's problems are probably more criminal than drug in nature. His overall score on the LCSF (12) suggests that he has been involved in, committed to, and identified with the criminal lifestyle for some time. His scores on the DLSI, on the other hand, suggest that he has less investment in a drug lifestyle (total DLSI score = 9) than he does in a criminal lifestyle and that his drug use may be a self-indulgent reflection of his criminal lifestyle. Support for this hypothesis can be found in the fact that social rule breaking was more heavily represented on Mark's DLSI than social rule bending (3 to 1). The results of the PICTS and PIDTS both suggest a strong criminal inclina-tion marked by frequent use of the cutoff (low frustration tolerance) and power orientation (high desire for control). However, just as it was impor-tant not to overlook criminal issues with Walter, it is equally vital that drug issues not be ignored with Mark since such experiences, even though they may have roots in criminal behavior, can rapidly become self-rein-forcing and independent of the contributing criminal lifestyle. Both lifestyles consequently need to be addressed in working with Mark, although the criminal lifestyle should probably be the focus of early inter-ventions. Some of the issues identified in this preliminary evaluation were incorporated into Mark's change plan. These included his tendency to disregard both the rights of others and the rules of society and his desire to be around those still involved with drugs and crime.

Intervention

Few people would argue against trying to intervene as soon as possible with a client. This, in fact, has given rise to an emphasis on juvenile interventions as a way of preventing adult crime and drug use. Some juveniles, however, are too far along in the lifestyle to benefit from preventive interventions. The difficulty in working with juveniles before they enter the adult prison system, but after they have begun to experience the benefits of a drug or criminal lifestyle, is that they are often less amenable to change than more experienced individuals. Their natural resiliency and the fact that they have yet to experience the full negative impact of the lifestyle work against them. This may also explain why Mark has progressed more slowly than had been hoped, given his above-average intelligence. Drugs and crime apparently still appeal to Mark, perhaps because he has not experienced the full negative ramifications of these behaviors. For this reason, Mark's change plan is weighted toward early phase issues such as the development of crises and the creation of a shaman effect. Among the crises identified by Mark were the harm he caused his adoptive mother and grandmother, not finishing college, not seeing his girlfriend, and hearing his adoptive mother cry during his sentencing. These crises were developed by buttressing Mark's imagery skills and teaching how to use these images to combat the urge to use drugs and commit crime. Mark's desire for social approval was used to encourage his participation in group sessions with older individuals who had already begun making changes in their lives and was nurtured by a growing therapeutic alliance with two therapists, one of whom was female. The creation of a shaman effect and the modeling of prosocial behavior were also critical aspects of Mark's change plan, as were several other general strategies such as analyzing crime-related movies and participating in the mentoring process, initially as a student and later as a mentor.

Mark's responses on the Fear Checklist suggest that he has fairly good insight into his fear, which reflects concerns over social acceptance, control, and identity, with a slightly greater emphasis on identity. It is speculated that much of Mark's anger is his reaction to this fear, and so while anger control training may benefit the client, it may also be necessary to teach him how to deal more effectively with his underlying fears and issues. A number of these fears were addressed in individual sessions with the primary therapist. In light of the role that identity appears to play in the genesis of Mark's fear, the Bipolar Identity Survey was administered, the results of which are reproduced in Figure 8.2. As Mark's

BIPOLAR IDENTITY SURVEY

1a. Three positive messages you recall receiving from your parents/caregivers
Never lie
Never steal
Respect

1b. Three negative messages you recall receiving from your parents/caregivers
Fighting (violence)
Power over others

2a. Two behaviors for which you were generously rewarded as a child
Good grades in school
Good behavior in school

2b. Two behaviors for which you were consistently punished as a child
Fighting
Being sneaky

3a. Favorite story as a child

3b. Story you disliked as child

4a. Favorite TV show during childhood
(American) *Gladiators*

4b. TV show you disliked as child
Soap operas

5a. A favorite movie
Cyborg

5b. A movie you did not like
(Invasion of) *Body snatchers*

6a. Two things you have accomplished in life that you are proud of
Surviving
College

6b. Two things you have done in life that you are ashamed of
Abusing my dog
Hurting a kid

7a. Two personal traits you see as positive
Sensitive
Head-strong

7b. Two personal traits you see as negative
Too head-strong at times
Fight too much

8a. Two things you are good at
Computers
Water skiing

8b. Two things you are bad at
Basketball
Baseball

9a. Two physical characteristics you like about yourself
Well muscled body
Long hair

9b. Two physical characteristics you do not like about yourself
Short
Freckles

10a. A nickname you like having others refer to you by
Thunder

10b. A nickname you have been referred to but which you resent
Shorty

11a. A single word that is likely to be used by someone attempting to describe your personality
real

11b. A single word that is unlikely to be used by someone attempting to describe your personality
Unreal

(continues over page)

Figure 8-2. Mark's responses on the bipolar identity survey. (Adapted and reproduced by kind permission of Taylor & Francis, © 1996.).

(continued)

12a. Two characteristics you have observed in others that attract you to them *Quiet* *Sensitive*	10b. Two characteristics you have observed in others that repulse you *Big mouths* *Liars*
13a. Three people you admire *Steven Segal* (actor) *James Hetfield* (rock star) *Edgar Allan Poe* (author)	13b. Three people you do not respect *Madonna* (entertainer) *Bill Clinton* (US President) *Janet Reno* (US Attorney Gen.)
14a. What you want people to remember you by *Strong, real, sensitive guy*	14b. What you don't want people to remember you by *Weak, fake, cold*

Figure 8.2. *(continued)*

responses indicate, he is a sensitive individual who prizes strength and honesty, yet is ready to fight in situations where he perceives that his manhood is being challenged or his short stature ridiculed. In fact, Mark has sought to avoid such disrespect by building his body and learning to fight. Given the fact that none of the six people listed on item 13 of the Bipolar Identity Survey (people you admire or don't respect) is anyone with whom Mark has had personal contact, there may be a serious lack of role models in his life. Encouraging movement beyond the initial phase of intervention, requires investigation beyond the surface issues (toughness, strength) that Mark has thrown up as a defensive shield. It is too early in the intervention to determine how well Mark will fare with his change plan, although his above-average intelligence and willingness to view adversity as a challenge bode well for future change as long as he can remain free of the criminal socialization experiences found in a maximum security penitentiary. Consequently, he must prevent his anger and social rule-breaking behavior from landing him in one of these "schools of higher criminal learning."

CONCLUSION

What therapists working with substance-abusing criminals can best offer their clients is themselves. Clients learn by observing the actions of others and for a therapist to model inflexibility, dogmatism, or bewilderment is to shine a negative light on one's intervention. Programs of assisted change are most effective when applied in a flexible, genuine, and competent manner and where scripting and fragmentation are kept to a minimum. General strategies and attitudes must therefore supplement, and in some cases supplant, the more easily administered specific strategies described in Chapters 5 through 7. The integration and melding of these two perspectives may produce the best results, keeping in mind that all change is, in the end, self-change. Accordingly, therapists and other helping professionals must come to terms with the fact that the power for change lies within the client and not within themselves. According to the founding tenets of lifestyle intervention, the therapist's job is to stimulate client responsibility, hope, and empowerment and instruct clients in basic skills designed to maintain preliminary changes in thinking and behavior. For a therapist to profess a belief in his or her own power to change a client is to engage in self-delusion of such magnitude that it shuts down legitimate opportunities for influencing clients.

References

Adlaf, E. M., Smart, R. G., Walsh, G. W., & Ivis, F. J. (1994). Is the association between drug use and delinquency weakening? *Addiction*, **89**, 1675–1681.

Akers, R. L. (1984). Delinquent behavior, drugs, and alcohol: What is the relationship? *Today's Delinquent*, **3**, 19–47.

Andersson, B., Nilsson, K., & Tunving, K. (1983). Drug careers in perspective. *Acta Psychiatrica Scandinavica*, **67**, 249–257.

Anglin, M. D., Brecht, M. L., Woodward, J. A., & Bonett, D. G. (1986). An empirical study of maturing out: Conditional factors. *International Journal of the Addictions*, **21**, 233–246.

Anglin, M. D., & Speckart, G. (1988). Narcotics and crime: A multisample, multimethod analysis. *Criminology*, **26**, 197–233.

Annis, H. M., & Chan, D. (1983). The differential treatment model: Empirical evidence from a personality typology of adult offenders. *Criminal Justice and Behavior*, **10**, 159–173.

Baily, R. C., Hser, Y.-I., Hsieh, S.-H., & Anglin, M. D. (1994). Influences affecting maintenance and cessation of narcotics addiction. *Journal of Drug Issues*, **24**, 249–272.

Bakan, D. (1996). Origination, self-determination, and psychology. *Journal of Humanistic Psychology*, **36**, 9–20.

Ball, J. C., Shaffer, J. W., & Nurco, D. N. (1985). The day-to-day criminality of heroin addicts in Baltimore—A study in the continuity of offence rates. *Drug and Alcohol Dependence*, **12**, 119–142.

Bandura, A. (1977). *Social learning theory*. Englewood Cliffs, NJ: Prentice Hall.

Barton, S. (1994). Chaos, self-organization, and psychology. *American Psychologist*, **49**, 5–14.

Bean, P. T., & Wilkinson, C. K. (1988). Drug taking, crime and the illicit supply system. *British Journal of Addiction*, **83**, 533–539.

Beatty, W. W., Katzung, V. M., Moreland, V. J., & Nixon, S. J. (1995). Neuropsychological performance of recently abstinent alcoholics and cocaine abusers. *Drug and Alcohol Dependence*, **37**, 247–253.

Beck, A. J., & Shipley, B. E. (1989). Recidivism of prisoners released in 1983. *Bureau of Justice Statistics Special Report* (NCJ-116261). Washington, DC: Bureau of Justice Statistics.

Beck, A. T., Wright, F. D., Newman, C. F., & Liese, B. S. (1993). *Cognitive therapy of substance abuse*. New York: Guilford.

Bennett, T. (1986). A decision-making approach to opioid addiction. In D. B. Cornish & R. V. Clarke (Eds.), *The reasoning criminal: Rational choice perspectives on offending* (pp. 83–103). New York: Springer-Verlag.

Biernacki, P. (1990). Recovering from opiate addiction without treatment: A summary. *NIDA Research Monograph Series*, **98**, 113–119.

Bigelow, G. E., Griffiths, R. R., & Liebson, I. A. (1977). Effects of response requirement upon human sedative self-administration and drug seeking behavior. *Pharmacology Biochemistry and Behavior*, **5**, 681–685.

Biron, L. L., Brochu, S., & Desjardins, L. (1995). The issue of drugs and crime among a sample of incarcerated women. *Deviant Behavior*, **16**, 25–43.

Blankfield, A. (1991). Women, alcohol dependence and crime. *Drug and Alcohol Dependence*, **27**, 185–190.

Booth, B. M., Russell, D. W., Soucek, S., & Laughlin, P. R. (1992). Social support and outcome of alcoholism treatment: An exploratory analysis. *American Journal of Drug and Alcohol Abuse*, **18**, 87–101.

Bradley, B. P., Phillips, G., Green, L., & Gossop, M. (1989). Circumstances surrounding the initial lapse to opiate use following detoxification. *British Journal of Psychiatry*, **154**, 354–359.

Brook, J. S., Whiteman, M. M., & Finch, S. (1992). Childhood aggression, adolescent delinquency, and drug use: A longitudinal study. *Journal of Genetic Psychology*, **153**, 369–383.

Bureau of Justice Statistics (1992). *Sourcebook of criminal justice statistics*. Washington, DC: Author.

Campanella, S. (1990). Delinquency and risk prediction. *Journal of Child and Youth Care*, **4**, 73–83.

Chait, L. D., Uhlenhuth, E. H., & Johanson, C. E. (1986). The discriminative stimulus and subjective effects of d-amphetamine, phenmetrazine and fenfluramine in humans. *Psychopharmacology*, **89**, 301–306.

Childress, A. R., McLellan, A. T., Ehrman, R., & O'Brien, C. P. (1987). Extinction of conditioned responses in abstinent cocaine or opioid users. *NIDA Research Monograph Series*, **76**, 189–195.

Childress, A. R., McLellan, A. T., & O'Brien, C. P. (1986). Conditioned responses in a methadone population: A comparison of laboratory, clinical, and natural setting. *Journal of Substance Abuse Treatment*, **3**, 173–179.

Clapper, R. L., Buka, S. L., Goldfield, E. C., Lipsitt, L. P., & Tsuang, M. T. (1995). Adolescent problem behaviors as predictors of adult alcohol diagnoses. *International Journal of the Addictions*, **30**, 507–523.

Clark, P. M. (1992). An experiment in employment of offenders: Enhanced employment development and social support (Doctoral dissertation, Michigan State University, 1992). *Dissertation Abstracts International*, **53**, 2A–627.

Cohen, T. (1979). Metaphor and the cultivation of intimacy. In S. Sacks (Ed.), *On metaphor* (pp. 1–10). Chicago, IL: University of Chicago Press.

Collins, R. L., & Lapp, W. M. (1991). Restraint and attributions: Evidence of the abstinence violation effect in alcohol consumption. *Cognitive Therapy and Research*, **15**, 69–84.

Condelli, W. S., & Hubbard, R. L. (1994). Relationship between time spent in treatment and client outcomes from therapeutic communities. *Journal of Substance Abuse Treatment*, **11**, 25–33.

Corless, T., & Dickerson, M. (1989). Gamblers' self-perceptions of the determinants of impaired control. *British Journal of Addiction*, **84**, 1527–1537.

Cowan, N. (1988). Evolving conceptions of memory storage, selective attention, and their mutual constraints within the human information-processing system. *Psychological Bulletin*, **104**, 163–191.

Cromwell, P. F., Olson, J. N., Avary, D. W., & Marks, A. (1991). How drugs affect decisions by burglars. *International Journal of Offender Therapy and Comparative Criminology*, **35**, 310–321.

Cusson, M., & Pinsonneault, H. P. (1986). The decision to give up cocaine. In D. Cornish & R. V. Clarke (Eds.), *The reasoning criminal: Rational choice perspectives on offending* (pp. 72–82). New York: Springer-Verlag.

Dance, K. A., & Kuiper, N. A. (1987). Self-schemata, social roles, and a self-worth contingency model of depression. *Motivation and Emotion*, **11**, 251–268.

Daniel, C. J. (1987). A stimulus satiation treatment programme with a young male fire setter. In B. J. McGork, D. M. Thornton, & M. Williams (Eds.), *Applying psychology to imprisonment: Theory and practice*. London: HMSO.

de Bono, E. (1977). *Lateral thinking: A textbook of creativity*. Markham, England: Penguin.

De Leon, G. (1989, October). *Therapeutic community research facts: What we know*. Paper presented at the What Works Conference, New York, NY.

DiClemente, C. C., Prochaska, J. O., Fairhurst, S. K., Velicer, W. F., Velasquez, M. M., & Rossi, J. S. (1991). The process of smoking cessation: An analysis of precontemplation, contemplation, and preparation stages of change. *Journal of Consulting and Clinical Psychology*, **59**, 295–304.

Dixon, T. M., & Baumeister, R. F. (1991). Escaping the self: The moderating effect of self-complexity. *Personality and Social Psychology Bulletin*, **17**, 363–368.

Donovan, M. E. (1984). A sociological analysis of commitment generation in Alcoholics Anonymous. *British Journal of Addiction*, **79**, 411–418.

Drummond, D. C., & Glautier, S. (1994). A controlled trial of cue exposure treatment in alcohol dependence. *Journal of Consulting and Clinical Psychology*, **62**, 809–817.

Ellis, A. (1970). *The essence of rational psychotherapy: A comprehensive approach to treatment*. New York: Institute of Rational Living.

Emrick, C. D., Lassen, C. L., & Edwards, M. T. (1977). Nonprofessional peers as therapeutic agents. In A. S. Gurman & A. M. Rozen (Eds.), *Effective psychotherapy* (pp. 120–160). New York: Pergamon.

Esbensen, F.-A., & Elliott, D. S. (1994). Continuity and discontinuity in illicit drug use: Patterns and antecedents. *Journal of Drug Issues*, **24**, 75–97.

Fagan, J., Weis, J. G., & Cheng, Y.-T. (1990). Delinquency and substance abuse among inner-city students. *Journal of Drug Issues*, **20**, 351–402.

Fanning, P. (1994). *Visualization for change* (2nd edn.). Oakland, CA: New Harbinger.

Farrell, A. D., & Danish, S. J. (1993). Peer drug associations and emotional restraint: Causes or consequences of adolescents' drug use? *Journal of Consulting and Clinical Psychology*, **61**, 327–334.

Farrell, A. D., Danish, S. J., & Howard, C. W. (1992). Relationship between drug use and other problem behaviors in urban adolescents. *Journal of Consulting and Clinical Psychology*, **60**, 705–712.

Faupel, C. E. (1987). Heroin use and criminal careers. *Qualitative Sociology*, **10**, 115–131.

Feinstein, D., & Krippner, S. (1988). *Personal mythology: The psychology of your evolving self*. Los Angeles: Jeremy P. Tarcher.

Felson, R. B., Ribner, S. A., & Siegel, M. S. (1984). Age and the effect of third parties during criminal violence. *Criminology*, **21**, 59–74.

Field, G. (1992). Oregon prison drug treatment programs. *NIDA Research Monograph Series*, **118**, 142–155.

Frank, J. D., & Frank, S. (1991). *Persuasion and healing: A comparative study of psychotherapy* (3rd edn.). Baltimore, MD: Johns Hopkins University Press.

Frankl, V. E. (1984). *Man's search for meaning: An introduction to logotherapy* (3rd edn.). New York: Simon & Schuster.

Freud, S. (1961). The ego and the id. In J. Strachey (Ed. and Trans.), *The standard edition of the complete psychological works of Sigmund Freud* (Vol. 19, pp. 3–66). London: Hogarth Press. (Original work published 1923.)

Gergen, K. (1985). The social constructionist movement in modern psychology. *American Psychologist*, **40**, 266–275.

Gibbs, J. J., & Shelly, P. L. (1982). Life in the fast lane: A retrospective view by commercial thieves. *Journal of Research in Crime and Delinquency*, **19**, 299–330.

Gleick, J. (1987). *Chaos: Making a new science*. New York: Viking.

Glover, E. (1960). *The roots of crime: Selected papers on psychoanalysis* (Vol. II). London: Imago.

Gorman, D. M. (1989). Is the 'new' problem drinking concept of Heather and Robertson more useful in advancing our scientific knowledge than the 'old' disease concept? *British Journal of Addiction*, **84**, 843–845.

Gottfredson, M. R., & Hirschi, T. (1990). *A general theory of crime*. Stanford, CA: Stanford University Press.

Green, B. T. (1981). An examination of the relationship between crime and substance abuse/use in a drug/alcohol treatment population. *International Journal of the Addictions*, **16**, 627–645.

Greenbaum, P. E., Brown, E. C., & Friedman, R. M. (1995). Alcohol expectancies among adolescents with conduct disorder: Prediction and mediation of drinking. *Addictive Behaviors*, **20**, 321–333.

Greenfield, T. K., & Weisner, C. (1995). Drinking problems and self-reported criminal behavior, arrests and convictions: 1990 US alcohol and 1989 county surveys. *Addiction*, **90**, 361–373.

Grilo, C. M., & Shiffman, S. (1994). Longitudinal investigation of the abstinence violation effect in binge eaters. *Journal of Consulting and Clinical Psychology*, **62**, 611–619.

Haines, P., & Ayliffe, G. (1991). Locus of control of behaviour: Is high externality associated with substance misuse? *British Journal of Addiction*, **86**, 1111–1117.

Hammersley, R., Forsyth, A., & Lavelle, T. (1990). The criminality of new drug users in Glasgow. *British Journal of Addiction*, **85**, 1583–1594.

Hammersley, R., & Morrison, V. (1987). Effects of polydrug use on the criminal activities of heroin users. *British Journal of Addiction*, **82**, 899–906.

Hanson, C. L., Henggeler, S. W., Haefele, W. F., & Rodick, J. D. (1984). Demographic, individual, and family relationship correlates of serious and repeated crime among adolescents and their siblings. *Journal of Consulting and Clinical Psychology*, **52**, 528–538.

Hare, R. D., McPherson, L. M., & Forth, A. E. (1988). Male psychopaths and their criminal careers. *Journal of Consulting and Clinical Psychology*, **56**, 710–714.

Hare-Mustin, R. T., & Marecek, J. (1988). The meaning of difference: Gender theory, post modernism and psychology. *American Psychologist*, **43**, 455–464.

Harlow, C. W. (1991). Drugs and jail inmates, 1989. *Bureau of Justice Statistics Special Report*. Washington, DC: Bureau of Justice Statistics.

98   Changing Lives of Crime and Drugs

Harrison, L., & Gfroerer, J. (1992). The intersection of drug use and criminal behavior: Results from the National Household Survey on Drug Abuse. *Crime and Delinquency*, **38**, 422–443.

Hawkins, J. D., Catalano, R. F., Gillmore, M. R., & Wells, E. A. (1989). Skills training for drug abusers: Generalization, maintenance, and effects on drug use. *Journal of Consulting and Clinical Psychology*, **57**, 559–563.

Heather, N., & Robertson, I. (1985). *Problem drinking: The new approach*. Harmondsworth, England: Penguin.

Henggeler, S. W., Borduin, C. M., Melton, G. B., Mann, B. J., Smith, L. A., Hall, J. A., Cone, L., & Fucci, B. R. (1991). Effects of multisystemic therapy on drug use and abuse in serious juvenile offenders: A progress report for two outcome studies. *Family Dynamics Addiction Quarterly*, **1**, 40–51.

Higgins, S. T., Budney, A. J., Bickel, W. K., & Badger, G. J. (1994). Participation of significant others in outpatient behavioral treatment predicts greater cocaine abstinence. *American Journal of Drug and Alcohol Abuse*, **20**, 47–56.

Hirschi, T. (1969). *Causes of delinquency*. Berkeley, CA: University of California Press.

Hirschi, T., & Gottfredson, M. (1983). Age and the explanation of crime. *American Journal of Sociology*, **89**, 552–584.

Hodgins, D. C., & Lightfoot, L. O. (1988). Types of male alcoholic and drug abusing incarcerated offenders. *British Journal of Addiction*, **83**, 1201–1213.

Hover, S., & Gaffney, L. R. (1991). The relationship between social skills and adolescent drinking. *Alcohol and Alcoholism*, **26**, 207–214.

Hubbard, R. L., Collins, J. J., Rachal, J. V., & Cavanaugh, E. R. (1988). The criminal justice client in drug abuse treatment. *NIDA Research Monograph Series*, **86**, 57–80.

Huselid, R. F., Self, E. A., & Gutierres, S. E. (1991). Predictors of successful completion of a halfway-house program for chemically-dependent women. *American Journal of Drug and Alcohol Abuse*, **17**, 89–101.

Ingram, J. A., & Salzberg, H. C. (1990). Effects of in vivo behavioral rehearsal on the learning of assertive behaviors with a substance abusing population. *Addictive Behaviors*, **15**, 189–194.

Jarvis, G., & Parker, H. (1989). Young heroin users and crime: How do the "new users" finance their habits? *British Journal of Criminology*, **29**, 175–185.

Jessor, R., & Jessor, S. L. (1977). *Problem behavior and psychosocial development: A longitudinal study of youth*. New York: Academic Press.

Jessor, R., Van Den Bos, J., Vanderryn, J., Costa, F. M., & Turbin, M. S. (1995). Protective factors in adolescent problem behavior: Moderator effects and developmental change. *Developmental Psychology*, **31**, 923–933.

Joe, G. W., Brown, B. S., & Simpson, D. D. (1995). Psychological problems and client engagement in methadone treatment. *Journal of Nervous and Mental Disease*, **183**, 704–710.

Johnson, B. D., Goldstein, P. G., Preble, E., Schmeidler, J., Lipton, D. S., Spunt, B., & Miller, T. (1985). *Taking care of business: The economics of crime by heroin abusers*. Lexington, MA: Lexington Books.

Kafka, M. P., & Prentky, R. (1992). A comparative study of nonparaphilic sexual addictions and paraphilias in men. *Journal of Clinical Psychiatry*, **53**, 345–350.

Kandel, D. B., & Raveis, V. H. (1989). Cessation of illicit drug use in young adulthood. *Archives of General Psychiatry*, **46**, 109–116.

Kanter, R. M. (1972). *Commitment and community: Communes and utopias in sociological perspective*. Cambridge, MA: Harvard University Press.

Khantzian, E. J. (1985). The self-medication hypothesis of addictive disorders: Focus on heroin and cocaine dependence. *American Journal of Psychiatry*, **142**, 1259–1264.

Kirmayer, L. J. (1993). Healing and the invention of metaphor: The effectiveness of symbols revisited. *Culture, Medicine, and Psychiatry*, **17**, 161–195.

Klingemann, H. K.-H. (1991). The motivation for change from problem alcohol and heroin use. *British Journal of Addiction*, **86**, 727–744.

Kokkevi, A., Liappas, J., Boukouvala, V., Alevizou, V., Anastassopoulou, E., & Stefanis, C. (1993). Criminality in a sample of drug abusers in Greece. *Drug and Alcohol Dependence*, **31**, 111–121.

Krippner, S. (1986). Dreams and the development of a personal mythology. *Journal of Mind and Behavior*, **7**, 449–462.

Krippner, S. (1994). Humanistic psychology and chaos theory: The third revolution and the third force. *Journal of Humanistic Psychology*, **34**, 48–61.

Kurtz, L. F. (1990). Twelve-step programs. In T. J. Powell (Ed.), *Working with self-help* (pp. 93–119). Silver Spring, MD: National Association of Social Workers.

Laessle, R. G., Tuschl, R. J., Waadt, S., & Pirke, K. M. (1989). The specific psychopathology of bulimia nervosa: A comparison with restrained and unrestrained (normal) eaters. *Journal of Consulting and Clinical Psychology*, **57**, 772–775.

Larson, J. D. (1992). Anger and aggression management techniques through the Think First curriculum. *Journal of Offender Rehabilitation*, **18**, 101–117.

Linville, P. W. (1987). Self-complexity as a cognitive buffer against stress-related illness and depression. *Journal of Personality and Social Psychology*, **52**, 663–676.

Litman, G. K., Stapleton, J., Oppenheim, A. N., Peleg, M., & Jackson, P. (1983). Situations related to alcoholism relapse. *British Journal of Addiction*, **78**, 381–389.

Lochman, J. E. (1992). Cognitive-behavioral intervention with aggressive boys: Three-year follow-up and preventive effects. *Journal of Consulting and Clinical Psychology*, **60**, 426–432.

Luthar, S. S., Glick, M., Zigler, E., & Rounsaville, B. J. (1993). Social competence among cocaine abusers: Moderating effects of comorbid diagnoses and gender. *American Journal of Drug and Alcohol Abuse*, **19**, 283–298.

MacDonald, J. E., & Gifford, R. (1989). Territorial cues and defensible space theory: The burglar's point of view. *Journal of Environmental Psychology*, **9**, 193–205.

Maddux, J. F., & Desmond, D. P. (1982). Residence relocation inhibits opioid dependence. *Archives of General Psychiatry*, **39**, 1313–1317.

Marlatt, G. A., & George, W. J. (1984). Relapse prevention: Introduction and overview of the model. *British Journal of Addiction*, **79**, 261–275.

Marlatt, G. A., & Gordon, J. R. (1980). Determinants of relapse: Implications for the maintenance of behavior change. In P. O. Davidson & S. M. Davidson (Eds.), *Behavioral medicine: Changing health lifestyles* (pp. 410–472). New York: Brunner/Mazel.

Marlatt, G. A., & Gordon, J. R. (Eds.) (1985). *Relapse prevention: Maintenance strategies in the treatment of addictive behaviors*. New York: Guilford.

Maultsby, M. C. (1975). *Help yourself to happiness through rational self-counseling*. New York: Institute for Rational Living.

McBride, D. C., Burgman-Habermehl, C., Alpert, J., & Chitwood, D. O. (1986). Drugs and homicide. *Bulletin of the New York Academy of Medicine*, **62**, 497–508.

McCusker, C. G., & Brown, K. (1990). Alcohol-predictive cues enhance tolerance to and precipitate "craving" for alcohol in social drinkers. *Journal of Studies on Alcohol*, **51**, 494–499.

McKay, J. R., Maisto, S. A., & O'Farrell, T. J. (1996). Alcoholics' perceptions of factors in the onset and termination of relapses and the maintenance of abstinence: Results from a 30-month follow-up. *Psychology of Addictive Behaviors*, **10**, 167–180.

McKay, J. R., Murphy, R. T., McGuire, J., Rivinus, T. R., & Maisto, S. A. (1992). Incarcerated adolescents' attributions for drug and alcohol use. *Addictive Behaviors*, **17**, 227–235.

McMullen, L. M. (1989). Use of figurative language in successful and unsuccessful cases of psychotherapy: Three comparisons. *Metaphor and Symbolic Activity*, **4**, 203–226.

McMurran, M. (1994). *The psychology of addiction*. Washington, DC: Taylor & Francis.

Menard, S., & Huizinga, D. (1989). Age, period, and cohort size effects on self-reported alcohol, marijuana, and polydrug use: Results from the National Youth Survey. *Social Science Research*, **18**, 174–194.

Menzies, R. G., & Clarke, J. C. (1995). The etiology of phobias: A nonassociative account. *Clinical Psychology Review*, **15**, 23–48.

Meyer, R. E., & Mirin, S. M. (1979). *The heroin stimulus: Implications for a theory of addiction*. New York: Plenum.

Miller, L. (1988). Neuropsychological perspectives on delinquency. *Behavioral Sciences & the Law*, **6**, 409–428.

Miller, P. M., & Eisler, R. M. (1977). Assertive behavior of alcoholics: A descriptive analysis. *Behavior Therapy*, **8**, 146–149.

Miller, W. R. (1985). Motivation for treatment: A review with special emphasis on alcoholism. *Psychological Bulletin*, **98**, 84–107.

Miller, W. R., Leckman, A. L., Delaney, H. D., & Tinkcom, M. (1992). Long-term follow-up of behavioral self-control training. *Journal of Studies on Alcohol*, **53**, 249–261.

Miller, W. R., & Rollnick, S. (1991). *Motivational interviewing: Preparing people to change addictive behavior*. New York: Guilford.

Modestin, J., & Ammann, R. (1995). Mental disorders and criminal behaviour. *British Journal of Psychiatry*, **166**, 667–675.

Monti, P. M., Abrams, D. B., Binkoff, J. A., & Zwick, W. R. (1986). Social skills training and substance abuse. In C. R. Hollin & P. Trower (Eds.), *Handbook of social skills training* (pp. 111–142). New York: Pergamon.

Najavits, L., & Strupp, H. (1994). Differences in the effectiveness of psychodynamic therapists: A process-outcome study. *Psychotherapy*, **31**, 114–123.

Nathan, P. E. (1988). The addictive personality is the behavior of the addict. *Journal of Consulting and Clinical Psychology*, **56**, 183–188.

National Institute of Justice. (1996). *1995 Drug Use Forecasting: Annual report on adult and juvenile arrestees*. Washington, DC: Author.

Newcomb, M. D., & McGee, L. (1989). Adolescent alcohol use and other delinquent behaviors: A one-year longitudinal analysis controlling for sensation seeking. *Criminal Justice and Behavior*, **16**, 345–369.

O'Brien, C. P., Childress, R., McLellan, T., & Ehrman, R. (1990). Integrating systematic cue exposure with standard treatment in recovering drug dependent patients. *Addictive Behaviors*, **15**, 355–365.

Ohannessian, C. M., Stabenau, J. R., & Hesselbrock, V. M. (1995). Childhood and adulthood temperament and problem behaviors and adulthood substance use. *Addictive Behaviors*, **20**, 77–86.

Oswald, L. M., Walker, G. C., Krajewski, K. J., & Reilly, E. L. (1994). General and specific locus of control in cocaine abusers. *Journal of Substance Abuse*, **6**, 179–190.

Oyserman, D., & Saltz, E. (1993). Competence, delinquency, and attempts to attain possible selves. *Journal of Personality and Social Psychology*, **65**, 360–374.

Palmer, T. (1991). The effectiveness of intervention: Recent trends and current issues. *Crime & Delinquency*, **37**, 330–346.

Peat, B. J., & Winfree, L. T. (1992). Reducing the intra-institutional effects of "prisonization": A study of a therapeutic community for drug-use inmates. *Criminal Justice and Behavior*, **19**, 206–225.

Pettiway, L. E., Dolinsky, S., & Grigoryan, A. (1994). The drug and criminal activity patterns of urban offenders: A Markov chain analysis. *Journal of Quantitative Criminology*, **10**, 79–107.

Piaget, J. (1963). The attainment of invariants and reversible operations in the development of thinking. *Social Research*, **30**, 283–299.

Pihl, R. O., & Peterson, J. (1995). Drugs and aggression: Correlations, crime and human manipulative studies and some proposed mechanisms. *Journal of Psychiatric Neuroscience*, **20**, 141–149.

Platt, J. J., & Hermalin, J. A. (1989). Social skill deficit interventions for substance abusers. *Psychology of Addictive Behaviors*, **3**, 114–133.

Preston, K. L., Bigelow, G. E., Bickel, W., & Liebson, I. A. (1987). Three-choice drug discrimination in opioid-dependent humans: Hydromorphone, naloxone and saline. *Journal of Pharmacology and Experimental Therapeutics*, **243**, 1002–1009.

Prochaska, J. O., & DiClemente, C. C. (1992). Stages of change in the modification of problem behaviors. In M. Hersen, R. M. Eisler, & P. M. Miller (Eds.), *Progress in behavior modification* (pp. 184–214). Sycamore, IL: Sycamore.

Project MATCH Research Group. (1993). Project MATCH: Rationale and methods for a multisite clinical trial matching patients to alcoholism treatment. *Alcoholism: Clinical and Experimental Research*, **17**, 1130–1145.

Quinsey, V. L., & Marshall, W. L. (1983). Procedures for reducing inappropriate sexual arousal. In J. G. Crew & I. R. Stuart (Eds.), *The sexual aggressor: Current perspectives on treatment* (pp. 267–289). New York: Van Nostrand.

Rogers, C. R. (1957). The necessary and sufficient conditions for therapeutic personality change. *Journal of Consulting Psychology*, **21**, 95–103.

Ross, R. R., & Fabiano, E. A. (1985). *Time to think: A cognitive model of delinquency prevention and offender rehabilitation*. Johnson City, TN: Institute of Social Sciences and Art.

Ryan, C., & Butters, N. (1983). Cognitive deficits in alcoholics. In B. Kissen & H. Begleiter (Eds.), *The biology of alcoholism* (Vol. 7, pp. 485–538). New York: Plenum.

Sanchez, J. E., & Johnson, B. D. (1987). Women and drugs–crime connection: Crime rates among drug abusing women at Rikers Island. *Journal of Psychoactive Drugs*, **17**, 205–216.

Schacter, D. L. (1994). Implicit knowledge: New perspectives on unconscious processes. In O. Sporns & G. Tononi (Eds.), *Selectionism and the brain* (pp. 271–284). San Diego: CA: Academic Press.

Shipley, T. E. (1988). Opponent-processes, stress, and attributions: Some implications for shamanism and the initiation of healing relationships. *Psychotherapy*, **25**, 593–603.

Shover, N. (1983). The later stages of ordinary property offender careers. *Social Problems*, **31**, 208–218.

Simpson, D. D., & Marsh, K. L. (1986). Relapse and recovery among opioid addicts 12 years after treatment. *NIDA Research Monograph Series*, **72**, 86–103.

Skafte, D. (1987). Video in groups: Implications for a social learning theory of the self. *International Journal of Group Psychotherapy*, **37**, 389–402.

Sorenson, A. M., & Brownfield, D. (1995). Adolescent drug use and a general theory of crime: An analysis of a theoretical integration. *Canadian Journal of Criminology*, **37**, 19–37.

Spunt, B., Brownstein, H., Goldstein, P., Fendrich, M., & Liberty, H. J. (1995). Drug use by homicide offenders. *Journal of Psychoactive Drugs*, **27**, 125–134.

Stacy, A. W., Ames, S. L., Sussman, S., & Dent, C. W. (1996). Implicit cognition in adolescent drug use. *Psychology of Addictive Behaviors*, **10**, 190–203.

Stall, R., & Biernacki, P. (1986). Spontaneous remission from the problematic use of substances: An inductive model derived from a comparative analysis of the alcohol, opiate, tobacco, and food/obesity literatures. *International Journal of the Addictions*, **21**, 1–23.

Stephens, R. C. (1971). *Relapse among narcotic addicts: An empirical test of labelling theory*. Unpublished doctoral dissertation, University of Wisconsin, Madison.

Stephens, R. C., & McBride, D. (1972). Becoming a street addict. *Human Organization*, **35**, 78–94.

Stice, E., & Barrera, M. (1995). A longitudinal examination of the reciprocal relations between perceived parenting and adolescents' substance use and externalizing behaviors. *Developmental Psychology*, **31**, 322–334.

Sutherland, E. H., & Cressey, D. R. (1978). *Principles of criminology* (10th edn.). New York: Harper & Row.

Thomas, C. W., & Peterson, D. M. (1977). *Prison organization and inmate subcultures*. Indianapolis, IN: Bobbs-Merrill.

Thornberry, T. P. (1987). Toward an interactional theory of delinquency. *Criminology*, **25**, 863–892.

Tuchfeld, B. S. (1981). Spontaneous remission in alcoholics: Empirical observations and theoretical implications. *Journal of Studies on Alcohol*, **42**, 626–641.

Tuchfeld, B. S., Clayton, R. R., & Logan, J. A. (1982). Alcohol, drug use, and delinquent and criminal behaviors among male adolescents and young adults. *Journal of Drug Issues*, **12**, 185–197.

Tunis, S., Austin, J., Morris, M., Handyman, P., & Bolyard, M. (1996). *Evaluation of drug treatment in local corrections*. Washington, DC: National Institute of Justice.

Vaillant, G. E. (1983). *The natural history of alcoholism*. Cambridge, MA: Harvard University Press.

Valdez, A., Kaplan, C. D., Curtis, R. L., & Yin, Z. (1995). Illegal drug use, alcohol and aggressive crime among Mexican-American and white male arrestees in San Antonio. *Journal of Psychoactive Drugs*, **27**, 135–143.

van Kamman, W. B., & Loeber, R. (1994). Are fluctuations in delinquent activities related to the onset and offset in juvenile illegal drug use and drug dealing? *Journal of Drug Issues*, **24**, 9–24.

Waisberg, J. L., & Porter, J. E. (1994). Purpose in life and outcome of treatment for alcohol dependence. *British Journal of Clinical Psychology*, **33**, 49–63.

Waldorf, D., Reinarman, C., & Murphy, S. (1991). *Cocaine changes: The experience of using and quitting*. Philadelphia: Temple University Press.

Walter, D., Nagoshi, C., Muntaner, C., & Haertzen, C. A. (1990). The prediction of drug dependence from expectancy for hostility while intoxicated. *International Journal of the Addictions*, **25**, 1151–1168.

Walters, G. D. (1990). *The criminal lifestyle: Patterns of serious criminal conduct*. Newbury Park, CA: Sage.

Walters, G. D. (1992). *Foundations of criminal science: Vol. 2. The use of knowledge*. New York: Praeger.

Walters, G. D. (1994a). Discriminating between high and low volume substance abusers by means of the Drug Lifestyle Screening Interview. *American Journal of Drug and Alcohol Abuse*, **20**, 19–33.

Walters, G. D. (1994b). *Escaping the journey to nowhere: The psychology of alcohol and other drug abuse*. Washington, DC: Taylor & Francis.

Walters, G. D. (1995a). Factor structure of the Lifestyle Criminality Screening Form. *International Journal of Offender Therapy and Comparative Criminology*, **39**, 99–108.

Walters, G. D. (1995b). Predictive validity of the Drug Lifestyle Screening Interview: A two-year follow-up. *American Journal of Drug and Alcohol Abuse*, **21**, 187–194.

Walters, G. D. (1995c). The Psychological Inventory of Criminal Thinking Styles: Part I. Reliability and preliminary validity. *Criminal Justice and Behavior*, **22**, 307–325.

Walters, G. D. (1996a). Addiction and identity: Exploring the possibility of a relationship. *Psychology of Addictive Behaviors*, **10**, 9–17.

Walters, G. D. (1996b). The natural history of substance misuse in an incarcerated criminal population. *Journal of Drug Issues*, **26**, 913–928.

Walters, G. D. (1996c). *Substance abuse and the new road to recovery: A practitioner's guide*. Washington, DC: Taylor & Francis.

Walters, G. D. (1997a). A confirmatory factor analysis of the Lifestyle Criminality Screening Form. *Criminal Justice and Behavior*, **24**, 294–308.

Walters, G. D. (1997b). The Shaman effect in substance abuse counseling. *Manuscript under review*.

Walters, G. D. (1998). *The addiction concept: Working hypothesis or self-fulfilling prophesy?* Boston: Allyn & Bacon.

Walters, G. D., & Chlumsky, M. L. (1993). The Lifestyle Criminality Screening Form and antisocial personality disorder: Predicting release outcome in a state prison sample. *Behavioral Sciences & the Law*, **11**, 111–115.

Walters, G. D., Revella, L., & Baltrusaitis, W. J. (1990). Predicting parole/probation outcome with the aid of the Lifestyle Criminality Screening Form. *Psychological Assessment*, **2**, 313–316.

Walters, G. D., White, T. W., & Denney, D. (1991). The Lifestyle Criminality Screening Form: Preliminary data. *Criminal Justice and Behavior*, **18**, 406–418.

Watts, W. D., & Wright, L. S. (1990). The relationship of alcohol, tobacco, marijuana, and other illicit drug use to delinquency among Mexican-American, black, and white adolescent males. *Adolescence*, **25**, 171–181.

Weaver, F. M., & Carroll, J. S. (1985). Crime perceptions in a natural setting by expert and novice shoplifters. *Social Psychology Quarterly*, **48**, 349–359.

Weiner, B. (Ed.) (1974). *Achievement motivation and attribution theory.* Morristown, NJ: General Learning Press.

Wexler, H. K., Falkin, G. P., Lipton, D. S., & Rosenblum, A. B. (1992). Outcome evaluation of a prison therapeutic community for substance abuse treatment. *NIDA Research Monograph Series,* **118**, 156–175.

White, H. R., & Labouvie, E. W. (1994). Generality versus specificity of problem behavior: Psychological and functional differences. *Journal of Drug Issues,* **24**, 44–74.

White, R. W. (1959). Motivation reconsidered: The concept of competence. *Psychological Review,* **66**, 297–323.

Wilson, J. Q., & Herrnstein, R. J. (1985). *Crime and human nature.* New York: Simon & Schuster.

Windle, M., & Miller, B. A. (1990). Problem drinking and depression among DWI offenders: A three-wave longitudinal study. *Journal of Consulting and Clinical Psychology,* **58**, 166–174.

Yochelson, S., & Samenow, S. E. (1976). *The criminal personality: Vol. 1. A profile for change.* New York: Jason Aronson.

Zimmer-Hofler, D., & Dobler-Mikola, A. (1992). Swiss heroin-addicted females: Career and social adjustment. *Journal of Substance Abuse Treatment,* **9**, 159–170.

Zimmerman, M. A., & Maton, K. I. (1992). Life-style and substance use among male African-American urban adolescents: A cluster analytic approach. *American Journal of Community Psychology,* **20**, 121–138.

Appendices

Lifestyle Criminality Screening Form—Revised

Section I. IRRESPONSIBILITY

A. Failed to provide child support for at least one biological child.

YES .... ☐ (1)

NO.. ☐ (0)

B. Terminated formal education prior to graduating from high school.

YES .... ☐ (1)

NO.. ☐ (0)

C. Longest job ever held.

Less than six months... ☐ (2)

At least six months but less than two years....................... ☐ (1)

Two or more years .... ☐ (0)

D. Terminated from job for irresponsibility/quit for no apparent reason.

Two or more times... ☐ (2)

Once.. ☐ (1)

None reported .... ☐ (0)

TOTAL IRRESPONSIBILITY ☐

Section II. SELF-INDULGENCE

A. History of drug or alcohol abuse.

YES .... ☐ (2)

NO.. ☐ (0)

B. Marital Background.

Two or more prior divorces .... ☐ (2)

One prior divorce/more than one separation .... ☐ (1)

Single but with illegitimate child.. ☐ (1)

Married, no divorces/single no children .... ☐ (0)

C. Physical Appearance (check only one box).
   More than four separate tattoos/tattoos on face or neck ... ☐ (2)
   Presence of one to four separate tattoos .... ☐ (1)
   No tattoos .... ☐ (0)

TOTAL SELF-INDULGENCE   ☐

Section III. INTERPERSONAL INTRUSIVENESS

A. Confining offense.
   Intrusive (e.g., murder, rape, robbery, B&E, assault) .... ☐ (1)
   Non-intrusive .... ☐ (0)

B. History of prior arrests for intrusive behavior (excluding instant offense).
   Three or more .... ☐ (2)
   One or two .... ☐ (1)
   None .... ☐ (0)

C. Use of weapon or threatened use of weapon during instant offense.
   YES .... ☐ (1)
   NO .... ☐ (0)

D. Physical abuse of significant others (primarily family members).
   YES .... ☐ (1)
   NO .... ☐ (0)

TOTAL INTERPERSONAL INTRUSIVENESS   ☐

Section IV. SOCIAL RULE BREAKING

A. Prior non-traffic violation arrests (excluding instant offense).
   Five or more .... ☐ (2)
   Two to four .... ☐ (1)
   One or none .... ☐ (0)

B. Age at time of first non-traffic arrest.
   14 years of age or younger .... ☐ (2)
   Older than 14 but younger than 19 .... ☐ (1)
   19 years of age or older .... ☐ (0)

C. History of disruptive behavior in school (e.g., suspensions).
   YES .... ☐ (1)
   NO .... ☐ (0)

TOTAL SOCIAL RULE BREAKING   ☐

TOTAL CUMULATIVE INDEX   ☐

Drug Lifestyle Screening Interview

I. Personal Data

Name _____ Reg. No._____ Sex _____

Age _____ Race _____ Education _____ Marital _____

Primary Drugs of Abuse _____

Additional Information _____

II. Irresponsibility/Pseudoresponsibility

a. Did you drop out of high school before completing the 12th grade? ___

b. Have you ever been fired from a job or quit a job without warning? ___

c. Have you ever gotten into trouble for not paying your bills? ___

d. Have you ever been cited for failure to pay child support? ___

e. Did you regularly neglect the psychological needs of loved ones? ___

Note: Responding Yes receives a score of 1 and responding No a score of 0.

Irresponsibility/Pseudoresponsibility Score ___

III. Stress–Coping Imbalance

a. On a scale from 1 to 3, 1 representing a low level of stress and 3 a high degree of stress, rate your level of stress:

1. Right before you began using drugs ___
2. After you had been using drugs for six months ___

b. How did you handle stress during the period you were using drugs?

_____

_____

Note: Score 2 points if subject responds by using drugs, 1 point if they report some other form of escapism, and 0 points if they appeared to use more effective coping strategies.

Stress–Coping Imbalance Score ___

IV. Interpersonal Triviality

a. Did you spend more time with drug users or non-drug users?
1. Before you started using drugs yourself ___
2. During the early stages of your drug usage ___
3. During the advanced stages of drug involvement ___

b. A ritual is a routinized pattern of behavior which accompanies use of a particular drug. Indicate the degree to which rituals were part of your use of drugs (check one of the options listed below):

Not at all ___ (0)
To a moderate degree ___ (1)
To a high degree ___ (2)

c. List the specific rituals individual engaged in while using drugs.

_____

_____

_____

d. Did you find yourself engaging in empty and meaningless con-versations ("bullshit") with other drug users once you became involved in regular drug usage? — Yes (1) — No (0)

Interpersonal Triviality Score ___

V. Social Rule Breaking/Bending

a. Have you ever engaged in the following behaviors (one point each):
1. panhandling ___ (SRBe)
2. burglary ___ (SRBr)
3. lying to family members in order to get money for drugs ___ (SRBe)
4. selling drugs ___ (SRBr)
5. suspension from school for misbehavior ___ (SRBr)

    6. acting as a go-between in a drug deal ___ (SRBe)

    7. writing bad checks, though you intended to cover the check later ___ (SRBe)

    8. taking money from mother's purse or father's wallet before age 14 ___ (SRBr)

  b. Age of onset: Rule Breaking ___   Rule Bending ___

Social Rule Breaking/Bending Score _____

TOTAL DLSI SCORE _____

© *Taylor & Francis, 1996; used with permission.*

Estimated Self-efficacy in Avoiding Drugs

Instructions: Imagine you are on the streets and you encounter the following situations. Rate the degree to which you believe you would be able to resist the urge to use drugs utilizing the 5-point scale provided below:

0 = No confidence (would avoid drugs less than 50% of the time)
1 = Mildly confident (would avoid drugs approx. 50 to 74% of the time)
2 = Moderately confident (would avoid drugs approx. 75 to 89% of the time)
3 = Highly confident (would avoid drugs approx. 90 to 99% of the time)
4 = Extremely confident (would avoid drugs 100% of the time)

PART A

1. You get fired from your job 4 3 2 1 0

2. You feel depressed or sad.. 4 3 2 1 0

3. You are "hassled" by a counselor at the center where you
   go for drug treatment follow-up...................................... 4 3 2 1 0

4. You feel overwhelmed by responsibilities........................ 4 3 2 1 0

5. You are bored 4 3 2 1 0

PART B

6. You feel good about "staying clean" for six months 4 3 2 1 0

7. You must speak in front of a group of ex-drug abusers
   about your recent success in remaining drug-free.......... 4 3 2 1 0

8. Someone whose opinion you respect tells you that it may
   be possible to "dabble" in drugs without becoming
   "addicted" or getting "caught up" 4 3 2 1 0

PART C

9. You watch a movie where people are using drugs in a way
   reminiscent of how you once used drugs 4 3 2 1 0

10. You walk by a corner where you used to "cop" drugs..... 4 3 2 1 0

11. You feel restless inside that reminds you of how you
    used to feel when you went without drugs for several
    days 4 3 2 1 0

12. You are in a conversation with someone you used drugs
    with in the past and they start reminiscing about a par-
    ticular drug experience you both went through several
    years back 4 3 2 1 0

PART D

13. You come across a large stash of drugs you had hidden
    so well you had forgotten about it for several years 4 3 2 1 0

14. You are told by a colleague at work that he or she knows
    where you can get some "really good" drugs................... 4 3 2 1 0

PART E

15. You receive pressure from a group of old friends to go
    with them to a bar or disco where you know there will
    be a lot of drugs and drinking 4 3 2 1 0

16. You feel lonely 4 3 2 1 0

17. You have trouble making new friends 4 3 2 1 0

18. You are approached by a former drug associate who
    states that he has been using drugs for "years" without
    any problems and that if you go out with him he will
    teach you the secret to his success 4 3 2 1 0

19. You are surrounded by a group of old drug associates who
    respond to your desire to remain drug-free as a sign that
    you are "selling out" to the system and so should no longer
    be trusted or be allowed to be part of their group 4 3 2 1 0

20. You pick up on subtle messages from the people you care
    about most that they believe it is just a matter of time
    before you start using drugs again.................................... 4 3 2 1 0

After completing all 20 items, add up the scores by section (A, B, C, D, & E) and total the
sections. Next, divide each section score by the number of items (e.g., 5 in the case of Section
A, 3 in the case of Section B, and so on) to obtain the average estimate per item and record
this figure on the line to the right of the = sign.

Score for Section A   ____ ÷ 5 = ____
Score for Section B   ____ ÷ 3 = ____
Score for Section C   ____ ÷ 4 = ____
Score for Section D   ____ ÷ 2 = ____
Score for Section E   ____ ÷ 6 = ____

TOTAL SCORE   ____ ÷ 20 = ____

Estimated Self-efficacy in Avoiding Crime

Instructions: Imagine you are on the streets and you encounter the following situations. Rate the degree to which you believe you would be able to resist the urge to engage in crime using the 5-point scale provided below:

0 = **No confidence (would avoid crime less than 50% of the time)**
1 = **Mildly confident (would avoid crime approx. 50 to 74% of the time)**
2 = **Moderately confident (would avoid crime approx. 75 to 89% of the time)**
3 = **Highly confident (would avoid crime approx. 90 to 99% of the time)**
4 = **Extremely confident (would avoid crime 100% of the time)**

PART A

1. You get fired from your job... 4 3 2 1 0

2. You feel depressed or sad... 4 3 2 1 0

3. You are "hassled" by a cop or probation officer 4 3 2 1 0

4. You feel overwhelmed by responsibilities........................ 4 3 2 1 0

5. You are bored 4 3 2 1 0

PART B

6. You feel good about "staying clean" for six months 4 3 2 1 0

7. You must speak in front of a group of ex-cons concerning your recent success in remaining crime-free............. 4 3 2 1 0

8. Someone whose opinion you respect tells you that it may be possible to "dabble" in crime without getting "caught up"... 4 3 2 1 0

PART C

9. You watch a movie that reminds you of a crime you once committed 4 3 2 1 0

10. You walk by a corner where you used to sell drugs, a bank you once robbed, or a store you once stole from 4 3 2 1 0

11. You feel restless inside like you used to just prior to committing a crime 4 3 2 1 0

12. You are in a conversation with someone you have committed crimes with in the past and they start reminiscing about a crime the two of you pulled off many years ago 4 3 2 1 0

PART D

13. You come across an "easy" target for crime (e.g., unlocked car containing a stereo system, unattended cash register) 4 3 2 1 0

14. You are told by a colleague at work that you could stand to make a great deal of money should you assist him with "ripping off" your employer 4 3 2 1 0

PART E

15. You receive pressure from a group of old friends to go with them to a bar or disco where you know there will be trouble 4 3 2 1 0

16. You feel lonely 4 3 2 1 0

17. You have trouble making new friends 4 3 2 1 0

18. You are approached by a former criminal associate with a criminal plan that he or she states "can't miss" 4 3 2 1 0

19. You are surrounded by a group of old criminal associates who respond to your desire to remain crime-free as a sign that you are "selling out" to the system and so should no longer be trusted or be allowed to be part of their group 4 3 2 1 0

20. You pick up on subtle messages from the people you care about most that they believe it is just a matter of time before you start committing crime again 4 3 2 1 0

Now that you have completed all 20 items add up the scores by section (A, B, C, D, & E) and then total the sections. Next, divide each section score by the number of items (e.g., 5 in the case of Section A, 3 in the case of Section B, and so on) to obtain the average, estimate per item and record this figure on the line to the right of the = sign

Score for Section A   ____ ÷ 5 = ____
Score for Section B   ____ ÷ 3 = ____
Score for Section C   ____ ÷ 4 = ____
Score for Section D   ____ ÷ 2 = ____
Score for Section E   ____ ÷ 6 = ____

TOTAL SCORE   ____ ÷ 20 = ____

Lifestyle Stress Test

Instructions: Rate each of the following 20 situations and issues in terms of how often you experienced each in the month in which you were most heavily involved with drugs (first column) and in the past 30 days (second column) using the following scale:

0 = **Never experience the situation.**
1 = **At least one time, but no more than once a week.**
2 = **Several times a week, but not daily.**
3 = **At least once a day.**

	Month used drugs most	Past 30 days
1. Money or financial concerns.		
2. Feeling irritated with other people.		
3. Setting goals or standards that you could not realistically achieve.		
4. Arguing with others about relatively trivial matters.		
5. Feeling that you have lost control over your life.		
6. Problems communicating with spouse, family, friends, or boss.		
7. Being saddled with too much responsibility.		
8. Feeling pressured at work to meet unrealistic deadlines or achieve beyond your capabilities.		

	Month used drugs most	Past 30 days
9. Worrying about things you have little control over.		
10. Having trouble accepting compliments.		
11. Not having sufficient time for hobbies, leisure, or recreation.		
12. Feeling "crowded" by others.		
13. Spending too much time sitting and not enough time exercising.		
14. Having trouble saying no to unrealistic requests from others.		
15. Trying to do too many things at one time.		
16. Getting into physical fights with others.		
17. Wanting to change your life but not knowing how.		
18. Sense of being overwhelmed by the noise created by others.		
19. Feeling bored.		
20. Being "put down" by others.		
TOTAL SCORE		
Personal score (odd-numbered items)		
Interpersonal score (even-numbered items)		

© *Taylor & Francis, 1996; Used with permission.*

Fear Checklist

Instructions: Check off issues and experiences that are or have been personal sources of apprehension and concern for you. Record the number of checks found in the first column (items 1, 4, 7, 10, 13, and 16) in the box marked bonding, the number of checks found in the second column (items 2, 5, 8, 11, 14, and 17) in the box marked orientation, and the number of checks found in the third column (items 3, 6, 9, 12, 15, and 18) in the box marked identity.

1. intimacy____

      2. loss of
         control____

            3. failure____

4. honesty____

      5. powerlessness____

            6. disapproval___

7. dating____

      8. inadequacy____

            9. insig-
               nificance____

10. social
    relations____

      11. rejection____

            12. other people's
               opinions____

13. closeness____

      14. weakness____

            15. success____

16. commitment ____

       17. vulnerability ____

              18. anonymity* ___

☐   ☐   ☐

Bonding   Orientation   Identity

*The state or quality of being unknown or obscure.

Multiple Options Analysis

Instructions: You will be asked to generate as many different options (up to a maximum of 9) for each of the following eight situations. You will be given one minute to respond to each item, one item at a time. It is important to keep in mind that the object of this exercise is to generate as many different alternative solutions and options as possible to each item.

1. You want to determine whether a book case will fit into a space between your sofa and desk but have no tape measure or ruler handy. List as many alternative options for making this determination as you can.

    1.
    2.
    3.
    4.
    5.
    6.
    7.
    8.
    9.

2. You go out to your car in the morning and notice that it won't start. You have to be at work, which is 10 miles away, for a very important meeting that starts in 30 minutes. List as many alternative options for dealing with this situation as you can.

1.
2.
3.
4.
5.
6.
7.
8.
9.

3. You are in town and someone you know approaches you for a "few dollars" so that she can buy food for her children. However, you know this individual has a serious drug problem and you suspect that she will use the money for drugs. List as many alternative options as come to mind in administering to this old acquaintance.

1.
2.
3.
4.
5.
6.
7.
8.
9.

4. You and another individual must move a 1000-pound safe from a truck in the street to the third floor of an office building with no elevator. List as many alternative options as you can so that you might accomplish this task.

1.
2.
3.
4.
5.
6.
7.
8.
9.

5. Entertaining a group of friends at an expensive restaurant you notice that you are $35 short of covering the bill (not including the tip). Furthermore, the restaurant does not take personal checks, will only accept American Express (which you do not have), and has no automatic teller machine. List as many alternative options as you can for correcting your oversight.

  1.
  2.
  3.
  4.
  5.
  6.
  7.
  8.
  9.

6. Somebody has broken the windows in the front of your house twice in the past month. You suspect a neighborhood teenager but have no solid evidence that he is the culprit. List as many alternative options as cross your mind for correcting this situation.

  1.
  2.
  3.
  4.
  5.
  6.
  7.
  8.
  9.

7. Your boss, who happens to be physically attracted to you but for whom you have no feelings in return, informs you that unless you engage in sexual relations with him/her you will be fired. List as many alternative options as you can for managing these unwelcome proposals.

  1.
  2.
  3.
  4.
  5.
  6.
  7.
  8.
  9.

8. You are divorced and your ex-wife (or ex-husband) has custody of the children. However, your ex-wife/ex-husband has a serious alcohol problem and you are concerned about the welfare of your two young children. List as many alternative options as come to mind for how you might handle this situation.

1.
2.
3.
4.
5.
6.
7.
8.
9.

Values Inventory

Instructions: Rate the value (0 = none, 1 = low, 2 = moderate, 3 = high) you (a) have placed, (b) currently place, and (c) would like to place on the following priorities and situations.

	(a) In the Past When Most Involved in Criminal Activity	(b) At the Present Time	(c) Future Ideal
1. family			
2. job			
3. sex			
4. knowledge			
5. sharing			
6. mastery			
7. pleasure			
8. education			
9. friends			
10. productivity			
11. excitement			
12. truth			
13. love			

	(a) In the Past When Most Involved in Criminal Activity	(b) At the Present Time	(c) Future Ideal
14. competence			
15. food			
16. insight			
17. loyalty			
18. achievement			
19. power			
20. wisdom			
Items 1 + 5 + 9 + 13 + 17			
Items 2 + 6 + 10 + 14 + 18			
Items 3 + 7 + 11 + 15 + 19			
Items 4 + 8 + 12 + 16 + 20			

© *Taylor & Francis, 1996; used with permission.*

Psychological Inventory of Criminal Thinking Styles

(Version 3.0)

Name _____ Reg. No. _____

Age ____ Sex ____ Race _____ Education _____ Marital _____

Confining Offense _____ Sentence _____

Directions: The following items if answered honestly, are designed to help you better understand your thinking and behavior. Please take the time to complete each of the 80 items on this inventory using the four-point scale defined below:

4 = strongly agree
3 = agree
2 = uncertain
1 = disagree

1. I will allow nothing to get in the way of me getting what I want... 4 3 2 1

2. I find myself blaming society and external circumstances for the problems I have had in life..................................... 4 3 2 1

3. My mind is free of any serious psychological problems or difficulties 4 3 2 1

4. Even though I may start out with the best of intentions I have trouble remaining focused and staying "on track".... 4 3 2 1

5. There is nothing I can't do if I try hard enough................. 4 3 2 1

6. When pressured by life's problems I have said "the hell with it" and followed this up by using drugs or engaging in crime.. 4 3 2 1

7. I see no reason to change my behavior at this point in my life.. 4 3 2 1

8. I have found myself blaming the victims of some of my crimes by saying things like "they deserved what they got" or "they should have known better" 4 3 2 1

9. One of the first things I consider in sizing up another person is whether they look strong or weak 4 3 2 1

10. I occasionally think of things too horrible to talk about.... 4 3 2 1

11. I am afraid of losing my mind 4 3 2 1

12. The way I look at it, I've paid my dues and am therefore justified in taking what I want 4 3 2 1

13. The more I got away with crime the more I thought there was no way the police or authorities would ever catch up with me.. 4 3 2 1

14. I believe that breaking the law is no big deal as long as you don't physically hurt someone 4 3 2 1

15. I have helped out friends and family with money acquired illegally 4 3 2 1

16. I am uncritical of my thoughts and ideas to the point that I ignore the problems and difficulties associated with these plans until it is too late 4 3 2 1

17. It is unfair that I have been imprisoned for my crimes when bank presidents, lawyers, and politicians get away with all sorts of illegal and unethical behavior every day................ 4 3 2 1

18. I find myself arguing with others over relatively trivial matters 4 3 2 1

19. I can honestly say that the welfare of my victims was something I took into account when I committed my crimes 4 3 2 1

20. When frustrated I find myself saying "fuck it" and then engaging in some irresponsible or irrational act 4 3 2 1

21. I have many fewer problems than other people.................. 4 3 2 1

22. Even when I got caught for a crime I would convince myself that there was no way they would convict me or send me to prison 4 3 2 1

23. I find myself taking shortcuts, even if I know these shortcuts will interfere with my ability to achieve certain long-term goals.. 4 3 2 1

24. When not in control of a situation I feel weak and helpless and experience a desire to exert power over others............ 4 3 2 1

25. Despite the criminal life I have led, deep down I am basically a good person... 4 3 2 1

26. I will frequently start an activity, project, or job but then never finish it... 4 3 2 1

27. I regularly hear voices and see visions which others do not hear or see... 4 3 2 1

28. When it's all said and done, society owes me...................... 4 3 2 1

29. I have said to myself more than once that if it wasn't for someone "snitching" on me I would have never gotten caught... 4 3 2 1

30. I tend to let things go which should probably be attended to, based on my belief that they will work themselves out... 4 3 2 1

31. I have used alcohol or drugs to eliminate fear or apprehension before committing a crime 4 3 2 1

32. I have made mistakes in life 4 3 2 1

33. On the streets I would tell myself I needed to rob or steal in order to continue living the life I had coming 4 3 2 1

34. I like to be on center stage in my relationships and conversations with others, controlling things as much as possible. 4 3 2 1

35. When questioned about my motives for engaging in crime, I have justified my behavior by pointing out how hard my life has been 4 3 2 1

36. I have trouble following through on good initial intentions 4 3 2 1

37. I find myself expressing tender feelings toward animals or little children in order to make myself feel better after committing a crime or engaging in irresponsible behavior 4 3 2 1

38. There have been times in my life when I felt I was above the law... 4 3 2 1

39. It seems that I have trouble concentrating on the simplest of tasks 4 3 2 1

40. I tend to act impulsively under stress 4 3 2 1

41. Why should I be made to appear worthless in front of friends and family when it is so easy to take from others.. 4 3 2 1

42. I have never had any regrets about living a life of crime... 4 3 2 1

43. I tend to put off until tomorrow what should have been done today 4 3 2 1

44. Although I have always realized that I might get caught for a crime, I would tell myself that there was "no way they would catch me *this time*" 4 3 2 1

45. I have justified selling drugs, burglarizing homes, or robbing banks by telling myself that if I didn't do it someone else would 4 3 2 1

46. I make it a point to read the financial section of the newspaper before turning to the sports page or entertainment section 4 3 2 1

47. People have difficulty understanding me because I tend to jump around from subject to subject when talking 4 3 2 1

48. I get at least four to five hours of sleep most nights 4 3 2 1

49. Nobody tells me what to do and if they try I will respond with intimidation, threats, or I might even get physically aggressive. 4 3 2 1

50. When I commit a crime or act irresponsibly I will perform a "good deed" or do something nice for someone as a way of making up for the harm I have caused 4 3 2 1

51. I have difficulty critically evaluating my thoughts, ideas, and plans 4 3 2 1

52. Nobody before or after can do it better than me because I am stronger, smarter, or slicker than most people 4 3 2 1

53. I have rationalized my irresponsible actions with such statements as "everybody else is doing it so why shouldn't I" 4 3 2 1

54. If challenged I will sometimes go along by saying "yeah, you're right," even when I know the other person is wrong, because it's easier than arguing with them about it 4 3 2 1

55. I am not seriously mentally ill 4 3 2 1

56. The way I look at it I'm not really a criminal because I never intended to hurt anyone. 4 3 2 1

57. I still find myself saying "the hell with working a regular job, I'll just take it" 4 3 2 1

58. I sometimes wish I could take back certain things I have said or done 4 3 2 1

59. Looking back over my life I can see now that I lacked direction and consistency of purpose 4 3 2 1

60. Strange odors, for which there is no explanation, come to me for no apparent reason 4 3 2 1

61. When on the streets I believed I could use drugs and avoid the negative consequences (addiction, compulsive use) that I observed in others 4 3 2 1

62. I tend to be rather easily sidetracked so that I rarely finish what I start 4 3 2 1

63. If there is a short-cut or easy way around something I will find it 4 3 2 1

64. I have trouble controlling my angry feelings 4 3 2 1

65. I believe that I am a special person and that my situation deserves special consideration 4 3 2 1

66. There is nothing worse than being seen as weak or helpless 4 3 2 1

67. I view the positive things I have done for others as making up for the negative things 4 3 2 1

68. Even when I set goals I frequently do not obtain them because I am distracted by events going on around me 4 3 2 1

69. I have never "blacked out" except perhaps when I was drunk or using drugs 4 3 2 1

70. When frustrated I will throw rational thought to the wind with such statements as "fuck it" or "the hell with it" 4 3 2 1

71. I have told myself that I would never have had to engage in crime if I had had a good job 4 3 2 1

72. I can see that my life would be more satisfying if I could learn to make better decisions 4 3 2 1

73. There have been times when I have felt entitled to break the law in order to pay for a vacation, new car, or expensive clothing that I told myself I needed 4 3 2 1

74. I rarely considered the consequences of my actions when I was in the community 4 3 2 1

75. A significant portion of my life on the streets was spent trying to control people and situations 4 3 2 1

76. When I first began breaking the law I was very cautious, but as time went by and I didn't get caught I became over-

confident and convinced myself that I could do just about anything and get away with it 4 3 2 1

77. As I look back on it now, I was a pretty good guy even though I was involved in crime.. 4 3 2 1

78. There have been times when I have made plans to do something with my family and then cancelled these plans so that I could hang out with my friends, use drugs, or commit crimes 4 3 2 1

79. I tend to push problems to the side rather than dealing with them 4 3 2 1

80. I have used good behavior (abstaining from crime for a period of time) or various situations (fight with a spouse) to give myself permission to commit a crime or engage in other irresponsible activities such as using drugs.............. 4 3 2 1

Psychological Inventory of Drug-based Thinking Styles

(Version 1.0)

Name _____ Facility _____

Age _____ Sex _____ Race _____ Education _____ Marital _____

Directions: The following items, if answered honestly, are designed to help you better understand your thinking and behavior. For the purposes of this inventory drug refers to both alcohol and various illegal substances used by the individual to achieve an altered state of consciousness. Please take the time to complete each of the 80 items on this inventory using the four-point scale defined below:

    4 = strongly agree
    3 = agree
    2 = uncertain
    1 = disagree

1. I will allow nothing to get in the way of me getting what I want.. 4 3 3 1

2. I find myself blaming society and external circumstances for the problems I have had in life....................................... 4 3 2 1

3. My mind is free of any serious psychological problems or difficulties 4 3 2 1

4. Even though I may start out with the best of intentions I have trouble remaining focused and staying "on track".... 4 3 2 1

5. There is nothing I can't do if I try hard enough................. 4 3 2 1

6. When pressured by life's problems I have said "the hell with it" and followed this up by using drugs..................... 4 3 2 1

7. I see no reason to change my behavior at this point in my life... 4 3 2 1

8. I have found myself blaming other people who have been hurt by my drug use by saying things like "they deserved what they got" or "they should have known better".......... 4 3 2 1

9. I use drugs in order to change the way I feel or manipulate my mood state........................ 4 3 2 1

10. I occasionally think of things too horrible to talk about.... 4 3 2 1

11. I am afraid of losing my mind............................. 4 3 2 1

12. The way I look at it, I've paid my dues and am therefore justified in taking what I want 4 3 2 1

13. The more I got away with drug use the more I thought there was no way my parents, spouse, or the authorities would ever catch up with me 4 3 2 1

14. I believe that using drugs is no big deal as long as you don't hurt other people in the process............................. 4 3 2 1

15. I have helped out friends and family with money I have acquired dishonestly............................. 4 3 2 1

16. I am uncritical of my thoughts and ideas to the point that I ignore the problems and difficulties associated with these plans until it is too late 4 3 2 1

17. It is unfair that I have been hassled for my use of drugs when bank presidents, lawyers, and politicians get away with all sorts of illegal and unethical behavior every day.. 4 3 2 1

18. I find myself arguing with others over relatively trivial matters............................. 4 3 2 1

19. I can honestly say that I took into account the feelings of other people even when I was using drugs heavily............. 4 3 2 1

20. When frustrated I find myself saying "fuck it" and then engaging in some irresponsible or irrational act 4 3 2 1

21. I have many fewer problems than other people.................. 4 3 2 1

22. Even when I got into trouble for using drugs I would convince myself that I didn't require any assistance because I could stop anytime I wanted............................. 4 3 2 1

23. I find myself taking shortcuts, even if I know these shortcuts will interfere with my ability to achieve certain long-term goals............................. 4 3 2 1

24. When not in control of a situation I feel weak and helpless and experience a desire to exert power over others............. 4 3 2 1

25. Despite the drug lifestyle I have led, deep down I am basically a good person.. 4 3 2 1

26. I will frequently start an activity, project, or job but then never finish it... 4 3 2 1

27. I regularly hear voices and see visions which others do not hear or see.. 4 3 2 1

28. When it's all said and done, society owes me....................... 4 3 2 1

29. I have said to myself more than once that if it wasn't for someone else's nosiness I would have never gotten into trouble for my drug use... 4 3 2 1

30. I tend to let things go which should probably be attended to, based on my belief that they will work themselves out 4 3 2 1

31. There have been times when I intended to limit myself to a few drinks or a small amount of drug only to end up drunk or stoned 4 3 2 1

32. I have made mistakes in life 4 3 2 1

33. Before entering treatment I would give myself permission to use drugs by telling myself that I needed the drugs to function 4 3 2 1

34. I like to be on center stage in my relationships and conversations with others, controlling things as much as possible.. 4 3 2 1

35. When questioned about my motives for engaging in drug use, I have justified my behavior by pointing out how hard my life has been 4 3 2 1

36. I have trouble following through on good initial intentions... 4 3 2 1

37. I find myself expressing tender feelings toward animals or little children in order to make myself feel better about my use of drugs... 4 3 2 1

38. There have been times in my life when I felt I was above the law... 4 3 2 1

39. It seems that I have trouble concentrating on the simplest of tasks 4 3 2 1

40. I tend to act impulsively under stress 4 3 2 1

41. Why should I be made to appear worthless in front of friends and family when it is so easy to take from others.. 4 3 2 1

42. I have never had any regrets about my drug lifestyle 4 3 2 1

43. I tend to put off until tomorrow what should have been done today 4 3 2 1

44. Although I have always realized that I might get into trouble for using drugs I would convince myself that there was no way I would get into trouble *this time* 4 3 2 1

45. I have justified my involvement in crime and other irresponsible acts by telling myself that I had no choice in that I was addicted to drugs 4 3 2 1

46. I make it a point to read the financial section of the newspaper before turning to the sports page or entertainment section 4 3 2 1

47. People have difficulty understanding me because I tend to jump around from subject to subject when talking 4 3 2 1

48. I get at least four to five hours of sleep most nights 4 3 2 1

49. Nobody tells me what to do and if they try I will respond with intimidation, threats, or I might even get physically aggressive 4 3 2 1

50. When I use drugs or act irresponsibly I will perform a "good deed" or do something nice for someone as a way of making up for the harm I have caused 4 3 2 1

51. I have difficulty critically evaluating my thoughts, ideas, and plans 4 3 2 1

52. Nobody before or after can do it better than me because I am stronger, smarter, or slicker than most people 4 3 2 1

53. I have rationalized my use of drugs with such statements as "everybody else is doing it so why shouldn't I" 4 3 2 1

54. If challenged I will sometimes go along by saying "yeah, you're right," even when I know the other person is wrong, because it's easier than arguing with them about it 4 3 2 1

55. I am not seriously mentally ill 4 3 2 1

56. The way I look at it I'm not really a bad person because I never intended to hurt anyone 4 3 2 1

57. I still find myself saying "the hell with working a regular job, I'll get high or drunk instead" 4 3 2 1

58. I sometimes wish I could take back certain things I have said or done 4 3 2 1

59. Looking back over my life I can see now that I lacked direction and consistency of purpose... 4 3 2 1

60. Strange odors, for which there is no explanation, come to me for no apparent reason 4 3 2 1

61. When on the streets I believed I could use drugs and avoid the negative consequences (addiction, compulsive use) that I observed in others 4 3 2 1

62. I tend to be rather easily sidetracked so that I rarely finish what I start 4 3 2 1

63. If there is a short-cut or easy way around something I will find it 4 3 2 1

64. I have trouble controlling my angry feelings 4 3 2 1

65. I believe that I am a special person and that my situation deserves special consideration 4 3 2 1

66. There is nothing worse than being seen as weak or helpless... 4 3 2 1

67. I view the positive things I have done for others as making up for the negative things... 4 3 2 1

68. Even when I set goals I frequently do not obtain them because I am distracted by events going on around me..... 4 3 2 1

69. I have never "blacked out" except perhaps when I was drunk or using drugs... 4 3 2 1

70. When frustrated I will throw rational thought to the wind with such statements as "fuck it" or "the hell with it"...... 4 3 2 1

71. I have told myself that I would never have had to use drugs if I didn't have such a stressful life 4 3 2 1

72. I can see that my life would be more satisfying if I could learn to make better decisions... 4 3 2 1

73. There have been times when I felt entitled to use drugs because of the way my life was going 4 3 2 1

74. I rarely considered the consequences of my actions when I was in the community... 4 3 2 1

75. A significant portion of my life on the streets was spent trying to control people and situations 4 3 2 1

76. When I first began using drugs I was very cautious, but as time went by and I didn't get into serious trouble I became overconfident and convinced myself that I could get away with just about anything... 4 3 2 1

77. As I look back on it now, I was a pretty good person even though I used drugs ....
....4 3 2 1

78. There have been times when I have made plans to do something with my family and then cancelled these plans so that I could hang out with my friends or use drugs 4 3 2 1

79. I tend to push problems to the side rather than dealing with them 4 3 2 1

80. I have used good behavior (abstaining from drug use for a period of time) or various situations (fight with a spouse) to give myself permission to use drugs and engage in other irresponsible acts.. 4 3 2 1

Scoring Criteria for the PICTS and PIDTS

1.	En	+	28.	En	+	55.	Cf	−
2.	Mo	+	29.	So	+	56.	Sn	+
3.	Cf	−	30.	Ci	+	57.	Co	+
4.	Ds	+	31.	Co	+	58.	Df	−
5.	So	+	32.	Df	−	59.	Ds	+
6.	Co	+	33.	En	+	60.	Cf	+
7.	Df	+	34.	Po	+	61.	So	+
8.	Mo	+	35.	Mo	+	62.	Ds	+
9.	Po	+	36.	Ds	+	63.	Ci	+
10.	Df	−	37.	Sn	+	64.	Co	+
11.	Cf	+	38.	En	+	65.	En	+
12.	En	+	39.	Cf	+	66.	Po	+
13.	So	+	40.	Co	+	67.	Sn	+
14.	Mo	+	41.	Po	+	68.	Ds	+
15.	Sn	+	42.	Df	+	69.	Cf	−
16.	Ci	+	43.	Ci	+	70.	Co	+
17.	Mo	+	44.	So	+	71.	Mo	+
18.	Po	+	45.	Mo	+	72.	Df	−
19.	Sn	+	46.	Df	+	73.	En	+
20.	Co	+	47.	Ds	+	74.	Ci	+
21.	Df	+	48.	Cf	−	75.	Po	+
22.	So	+	49.	Po	+	76.	So	+
23.	Ci	+	50.	Sn	+	77.	Sn	+
24.	Po	+	51.	Ci	+	78.	Ds	+
25.	Sn	+	52.	So	+	79.	Co	+
26.	Ds	+	53.	Mo	+	80.	En	+
27.	Cf	+	54.	Ci	+			

Note: + scoring direction; strongly agree = 4, agree = 3, uncertain = 2, disagree = 1; − scoring direction: strongly agree = 1, agree = 2, uncertain = 3, disagree = 1. For the meaning of abbreviations, *see* Figure 4.1.

Bipolar Identity Survey

1a. Three positive messages you recall receiving from your parents/caregivers

_____

_____

_____

1b. Three negative messages you recall receiving from your parents/caregivers

_____

_____

_____

2a. Two behaviors for which you were generously rewarded as a child

_____

_____

2b. Two behaviors for which you were consistently punished as a child

_____

_____

3a. Favorite story as a child

_____

3b. Story you disliked as a child

_____

4a. Favorite TV show during childhood

_____

4b. TV show you disliked as a child

_____

5a. A favorite movie

_____

5b. A movie you did not like

_____

6a. Two things you have accomplished in life that you are proud of

_____

_____

6b. Two things you have done in life that you are ashamed of

_____

_____

7a. Two personal traits you see as positive

_____

_____

7b. Two personal traits you see as negative

_____

_____

8a. Two things you are good at

_____

_____

8b. Two things you are bad at

_____

_____

9a. Two physical characteristics you like about yourself

_____

_____

9b. Two physical characteristics you do not like about yourself

_____

_____

10a. A nickname you like having others refer to you by

_____

10b. A nickname you have been referred to but which you resent

_____

11a. A single word that is likely to be used by someone attempting to describe your personality

_____

11b. A single word that is unlikely to be used by someone attempting to describe your personality

_____

12a. Two characteristics you have observed in others that attract you to them

_____

_____

12b. Two characteristics you have observed in others that repulse you

_____

_____

13a. Three people you admire

_____

_____

_____

13b. Three people you do not respect

_____

_____

_____

14a. What you want people to remember you by

_____

14b. What you don't want people to remember you by

_____

Index

Related titles of interest...

Offender Profiling
Theory, Research and Practice
Janet L. Jackson and Debra A. Bekerian
Explores the role of offender profiling in criminal investigations and supporting a legal case.
Wiley Series in Psychology of Crime, Policing & Law
0-471-97564-8   254pp   1997   Hardback
0-471-97565-6   254pp   1997   Paperback

Crime, The Media and the Law
Dennis Howitt
Looks at the role of the mass media in legal and criminal processes.
Wiley Series in Psychology of Crime, Policing & Law
0-471-96905-2   225pp   1998   Hardback
0-471-97834-5   225pp   1998   Paperback

Therapeutic Communities for Offenders
Eric Cullen, Lawrence Jones and Roland Woodward
Summarises examples of 'best practice' that therapeutic communities can offer to offenders in the UK, Europe and the United States.
Wiley Series in Offender Rehabilitation
0-471-96545-6   296pp   1997   Hardback
0-471-96980-X   296pp   1997   Paperback

Making Sense with Offenders
Personal Constructs, Therapy and Change
Julia C. Houston
Informs about the application of personal construct theory to offenders, enabling practitioners to use this approach in their assessment and treatment of a wide range of offending behaviour.
Wiley Series in Offender Rehabilitation
0-471-95415-2   288pp   1998   Hardback
0-471-96627-4   288pp   1998   Paperback